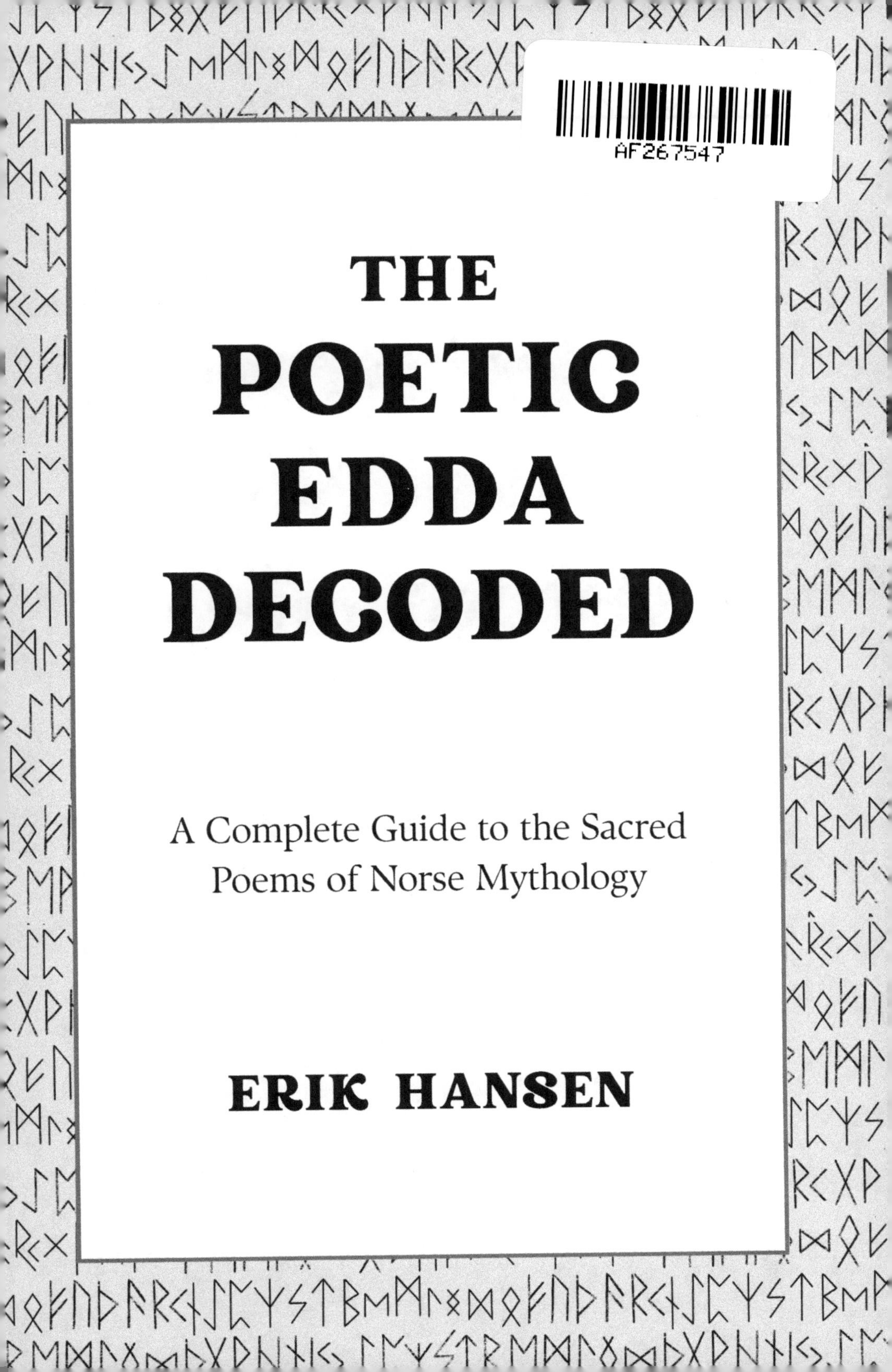

THE POETIC EDDA DECODED

A Complete Guide to the Sacred Poems of Norse Mythology

ERIK HANSEN

For permission requests, please contact:
Novus Liber Publishing
Email: info@yourbookshelf.top

First edition April 2026

Paperback ISBN 978-1-971761-04-6
eBook ISBN 978-1-971761-06-0

Contents

Author's Note

If you've read the Prose Edda, you already know the stories. You know Odin hung on the World Tree for nine days to win the runes. You know how the gods built Asgard's walls and what it cost them. You know the shape of Ragnarök — the wolf, the serpent, the fire, the silence after.

What you may not know is where Snorri Sturluson got all of it.

The Prose Edda, written around 1220, is a brilliant book. It is also, in a specific and important sense, a secondary source. Snorri was a Christian Icelandic scholar who wanted to preserve the old poetic vocabulary — the kennings, the mythological references, the whole elaborate machinery of skaldic verse — so that future poets wouldn't lose access to it. To do that, he retold the myths in prose, as context. His

Edda is a manual. A grammar. An act of conservation by someone who loved the material and understood, with some urgency, that it was slipping away.

The poems he was conserving are what you're holding now.

The Poetic Edda — the collection of mythological and heroic verse that Snorri drew from — is the source behind the source. These are the texts Snorri read, paraphrased, and quoted. Some of them were already centuries old when he was born. They are rougher than his prose, more elliptical, less interested in explaining themselves. They presuppose an audience that already knows the world they describe, which means reading them today requires a different kind of attention — slower, more lateral, willing to sit with gaps.

That difficulty is not incidental. It's the point.

When Snorri retells the myth of Sigurðr, he smooths it into narrative. When the Poetic Edda tells it, you get a dying dragon delivering a philosophical monologue, a valkyrie teaching runic magic to the man she loves, and a woman serving her murdered husband's killers their own sons for dinner — all in fragments, all without apology, all trusting you to understand why these things belong in the same story. The Prose Edda tells you what happened. The Poetic Edda makes you feel the weight of it.

This book is the part of a five-volume series on Norse paganism — a project that has moved through the mythology, the living practice of Asatru, the runes, and the Prose Edda — and arrives here at the oldest layer of the tradition. Each volume has tried to do the same thing: take material that can seem remote or exotic or merely decorative and show why it still carries force. You don't need to have read the others to read this one. Every chapter stands on its own, and you can move through the book in order or go straight to the poems that call to you. But if you've made the journey from the beginning, you'll recognize the territory — and find it stranger than you remembered.

That's as it should be. We're closer to the source now.

Introduction

Why These Poems Still Matter

Iceland, 1643. A bishop named Brynjólfur Sveinsson receives a manuscript.

Nobody knows where it came from. Nobody knows who owned it before, or how it survived the previous four centuries — the fires, the floods, the slow attrition of parchment in a damp climate, the indifference of people who had other things to worry about. It is a small book, as books go. Forty-five poems, written in a careful hand around 1270, containing material far older than that. The bishop recognizes immediately what he's holding. He calls it the Edda. He believes, wrongly but forgivably, that it was written by the historian Sæmundr the Wise in the twelfth century. He is wrong about the author and right about the importance.

That manuscript — the Codex Regius, the King's Book — is the reason you're reading this. Not because it was the only copy of these poems. Fragments existed elsewhere, scattered across other collections, quoted in other texts. But the Codex Regius was the concentration — the place where someone, at some point in the thirteenth century, had gathered the essential poems of the Norse mythological and heroic tradition and written them down in sequence, as if understanding that the tradition needed a container or it would dissolve. By 1643 the old religion had been dead in Iceland for six hundred years. The poems had outlasted the faith that produced them, the culture that performed them, and every political structure that had risen and fallen in between.

That's the first thing to understand about these texts: they are survivors, and survival at this scale is never accidental.

The second thing is harder to articulate but more important to feel. These poems are not interesting because they are old. They are interesting because they describe a way of being in the world that has no modern equivalent and that speaks, with startling directness, to experiences that are entirely modern. The certainty of loss and the decision to act anyway. The cost of knowledge — what you have to give up, what you have to become, to understand something true. The particular loneliness of seeing clearly in a world that prefers comfortable fictions. The question of what holds when everything else is taken away.

The Norse called that last thing drengskapr — something between honor and integrity and the refusal to become less than you are under pressure. The Poetic Edda doesn't define it. It shows it, over and over, in gods who know they will lose and fight anyway, in heroes who walk into destruction with their eyes open, in women who outlive every person they loved and keep moving.

This is not antiquarian material. It is a map. The territory it describes is one you already live in.

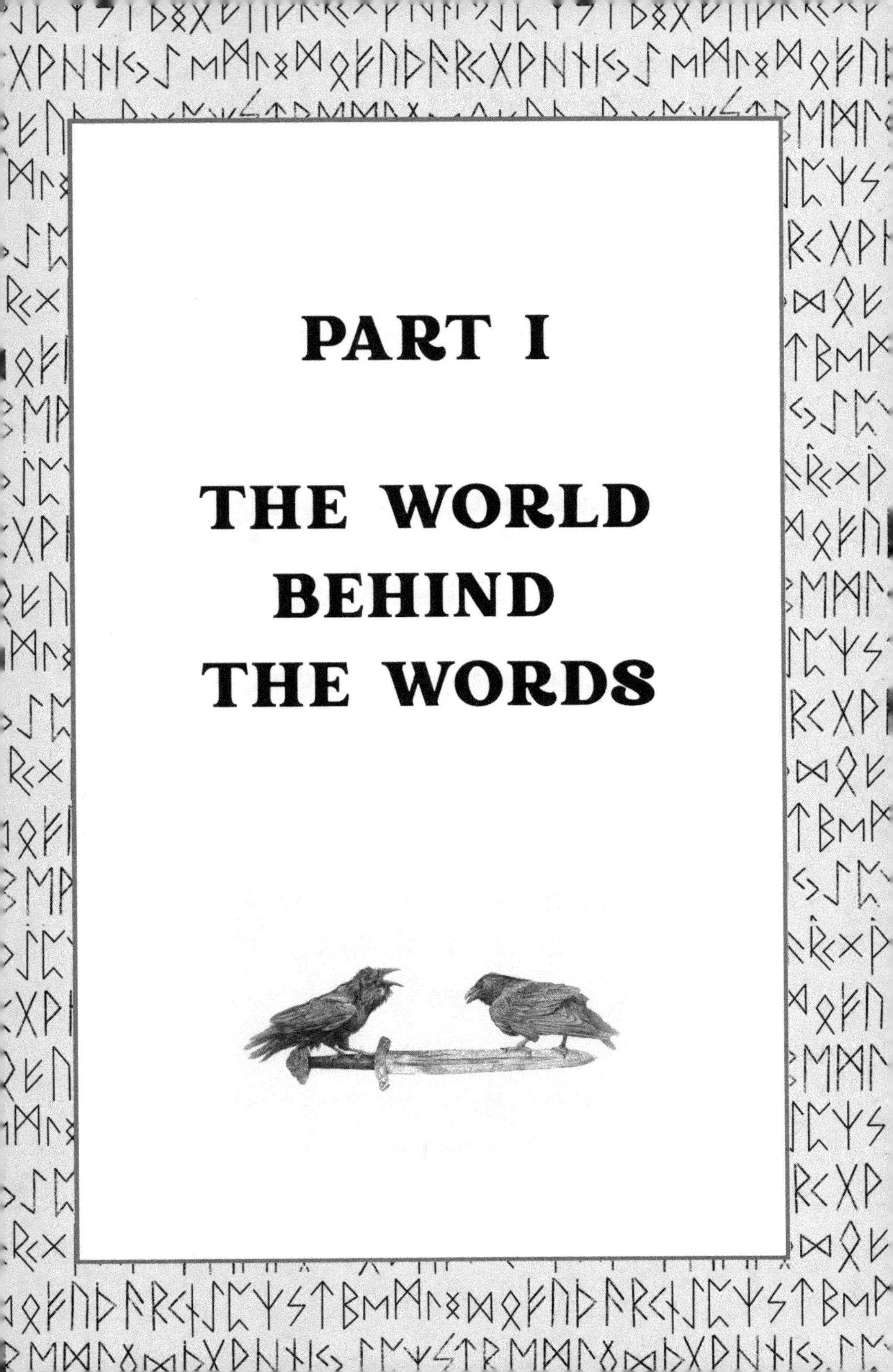

PART I

THE WORLD BEHIND THE WORDS

Chapter 1

What Is the Poetic Edda?

The Codex Regius is smaller than you'd expect. Roughly the size of a modern paperback, 45 leaves of calf vellum, written in a single hand — a careful, practiced hand, not a hurried one — sometime around 1270. It lived in Iceland for centuries, passed between owners whose names we mostly don't know, until Bishop Brynjólfur acquired it in 1643 and began telling people it was one of the most important manuscripts in existence. He was right. In 1662 he sent it to the King of Denmark in Copenhagen, which is why it's called the Codex Regius — the King's Book. It sat in the Royal Library for three hundred years. Iceland got it back in 1971, transported by naval vessel with the kind of ceremony usually reserved for the repatriation of human remains. The Icelandic government had been requesting its return since the 1940s. When the ship finally docked in Reykjavik, thousands of people lined the harbor.

What the manuscript contains is not a book in the modern sense — not a single work with a single author and a coherent plan. It's a collection. Forty-five poems, or the remains of forty-five poems, gathered by an unknown compiler who had reasons for the choices he made but didn't leave notes explaining them. The poems cover an enormous range: creation myths and apocalypse prophecy, cosmological catalogues, wisdom literature, heroic tragedy, divine comedy. Some are spare and ancient, compressed to the point of obscurity. Others are expansive, almost novelistic. They were composed at different times, in different places, by different people — and then, at some point in the thirteenth century, someone decided they belonged together.

That decision is the Poetic Edda.

A Title That Stuck

Before going further, the title needs to be addressed — because it's almost certainly wrong, and understanding why tells you something useful about the whole tradition.

"Edda" is what Bishop Brynjólfur wrote on the manuscript when he received it. He believed the poems had been composed or compiled by Sæmundr Sigfússon, an Icelandic scholar and priest who lived from 1056 to 1133, and he titled it accordingly: Edda Sæmundi multiscii — the Edda of Sæmundr the Wise. Neither part of this attribution is correct. Sæmundr almost certainly had nothing to do with it, and "Edda" was not a title the compiler gave the work. It was a word already in use — Snorri Sturluson had used it for his own work a generation earlier — and its meaning is genuinely disputed. It might derive from óðr, the Old Norse word for poetry or inspired mental activity, which would make "Edda" something like "the poetics." It might derive from the place name Oddi, where Sæmundr lived, which would make it a geographical attribution that got detached from its original meaning. It might simply mean "great-grandmother" — the old woman who tells the stories.

That last etymology is the one worth sitting with. If the word does mean great-grandmother, then the title is not a label but a description: these are the poems that come from the oldest voice in the room, the one who remembers what everyone else has forgotten. Whether or not the etymology is correct, it captures something true about how the Poetic Edda functions. It is prior. It is the memory behind the memory.

None of these etymologies is proven. The word stuck anyway — and with it, unfortunately, the title "Sæmundr's Edda" or "Elder Edda," implying that this collection is older than Snorri's Prose Edda, which happens to be true in terms of the material but not necessarily in terms of when it was compiled. The safer term, and the one most scholars now use, is simply the Poetic Edda, which describes what it is — a collection of Old Norse poetry — without making claims about authorship or priority that can't be supported.

Other Voices, Other Manuscripts

The Codex Regius is the primary manuscript, but not the only one.

AM 748, a smaller and later collection housed in the Arnamagnæan Institute in Reykjavik, preserves several mythological poems either not found in the Codex Regius or in different versions. The Hauksbók — compiled by the Icelandic lawyer and scholar Haukr Erlendsson in the early fourteenth century — contains a version of the Völuspá, the great prophetic poem that opens the Codex Regius, with significant variants. Other poems appear in the Flateyjarbók, in the Codex Wormianus, scattered through kings' sagas and mythological sagas as citations or embedded narratives. The Poetic Edda, as scholars study it today, is an editorial construction — a decision about which poems belong together — built primarily on the Codex Regius and supplemented from these other sources.

The construction has a hole in it.

Eight pages are missing from the Codex Regius. They were cut out — or fell out, or were removed — at some unknown point, and they fall in exactly the worst possible place: right in the middle of the heroic cycle, between the mythological poems and the heroic ones. What was on those pages is gone. Scholars call it the lacuna, the great gap, and they've spent considerable energy speculating about what it contained. The most plausible guess is that it held additional poems about Sigurðr — the Norse equivalent of Siegfried, the central hero of the Germanic tradition — that would have bridged the transition from the mythological section more smoothly than the abrupt jump we now have. The effect, as the heroic cycle stands, is of arriving mid-sentence. The world of gods ends; the world of heroes begins; and the seam between them is a wound. We'll never know for certain what filled it. The gap is permanent.

This is, in its way, appropriate. The Poetic Edda has always been a collection of fragments — voices speaking across enormous distances of time, preserved by accident and devotion and a series of lucky survivals. The missing pages are just the most visible expression of something that's true of the whole.

Snorri's Shadow

The difference between the Poetic Edda and the Prose Edda is not just a matter of format — prose versus verse — though that matters enormously. It's a difference in posture, in purpose, and in historical moment.

Snorri Sturluson wrote the Prose Edda around 1220. He was a Christian. Iceland had been officially Christian since the year 1000, which means that by Snorri's time the conversion was already two centuries old — long enough that the old religion had become, for most people, history and mythology rather than living practice. Snorri approached the myths the way a Renaissance humanist might approach classical mythology: as a cultural inheritance worth preserving, full of poetic and narrative richness, but not literally true. He retells the stories of Odin and Thor and Loki with obvious enthusiasm and considerable skill, but he frames them carefully — explaining, in his prologue, that the Norse gods were actually great human kings and warriors from Troy who were later divinized by a credulous population. This is euhemerism, the standard medieval Christian strategy for making pagan material safe. Snorri loved the myths. He also needed them not to be true.

The poems of the Poetic Edda were not written with that framing. Most of them predate the conversion, or at least predate the point at which Christian thought had fully colonized the imaginative world of Norse poetry. They don't explain themselves. They don't apologize for the gods. They don't offer alternative interpretations. Odin is Odin — the god who hung on the World Tree, who gave his eye for wisdom, who will die in the jaws of the Fenrir wolf and whose death is not a metaphor for anything. The cosmology is not allegory. The magic is real magic. When a völva — a seeress — is called up from the dead and asked to prophesy, the poem treats this as something that actually happens, not as a literary device.

The Prose Edda is a love letter to a tradition its author knew was dying. The Poetic Edda is the tradition itself, still breathing.

Gods First, Heroes Second

The Codex Regius divides its contents into two broad categories, and the division is worth understanding before you read a single poem.

Thirteen poems make up the mythological section — dealing with the gods, the cosmos, the creation and destruction of the world. These are the poems that give us our clearest picture of Norse religious thought: the structure of the universe, the relationships between the divine families, the nature of fate and time, the mechanics of magic. The Völuspá opens the collection; the Hymiskviða and Þrymskviða close it out with Thor poems that function almost as comic relief after the cosmic weight of what came before.

What follows is the heroic section — poems about human (or semi-human) warriors, their loves and feuds and deaths. These are organized around two main cycles: the Helgi poems, dealing with a legendary Norse warrior and his valkyrie lover, and the Völsung cycle, the sprawling tragedy of Sigurðr and Brynhildr and Guðrún that forms the Norse version of what the Germans later called the Nibelungenlied. The heroic poems are longer, more narrative, more novelistic in feel — but they share the same cosmological assumptions as the mythological section. Fate operates with the same implacable logic. The difference is that in the heroic poems, it's human beings who have to live inside that logic, without the consolation of divine power.

The compiler arranged these sections deliberately. Reading the book in order — myths first, heroes second — creates a specific effect: by the time you reach the Völsung cycle, you've already been told how the world ends. The heroic tragedies don't need to announce themselves as tragic. The reader already knows the shape of things.

Layers

When were these poems written? The honest answer is: we don't know, and the question is more complicated than it looks.

The Codex Regius was copied around 1270. That's a fixed point. But copying is not composing — the poems in the manuscript are older than the manuscript itself, some of them substantially older. Linguistic analysis, metrical patterns, and historical references allow scholars to place rough brackets around the dating, but those brackets are wide.

The oldest poems in the corpus — the Atlakviða, the Hamðismál, possibly the Völuspá in some form — may date to the ninth century, or even earlier in terms of the oral traditions that fed them. Oral tradition complicates the dating question further: a poem can preserve archaic linguistic features not because it was composed early, but because it was transmitted conservatively, with audiences and performers who prized the old forms. The Völsung cycle, in the shape preserved in the Codex Regius, probably reached something like its current form between the tenth and twelfth centuries. Other poems, particularly some of the more didactic mythological ones, show signs of later composition — their language is smoother, their cosmology more systematized, their apparent familiarity with Christian concepts of the afterlife more pronounced.

What this means in practice is that the Poetic Edda is not a snapshot of a single moment. It's a stratigraphic record — layers of composition and transmission compressed into a single manuscript, with the older layers visible beneath the newer ones if you know where to look. Reading it as a unified text, as this book mostly does, requires a certain willingness to paper over those layers. Reading it as a historical document requires pulling them apart. Both approaches are legitimate. This book is primarily interested in the first, while keeping the second in view.

The geographic question is similarly unresolved. Norwegian or Icelandic? Probably both. Norse poetry was not confined to a single location — it traveled with the people who carried it, from Norway to Iceland to the British Isles to the Norman settlements in France. Some poems almost certainly originated in Norway and were preserved in Iceland after Norway's conversion to Christianity made them less welcome in their homeland. Iceland's geographic isolation and its strong antiquarian culture made it the natural archive for material that might otherwise have been lost. The Icelanders knew what they were doing when they wrote these things down. They were keeping something alive.

What the Corpus Is

The word "corpus" — the Latin term scholars use for a body of related texts — implies a coherence that the Poetic Edda only partially has. The boundaries of the corpus shift depending on who's drawing them. Include every poem that shares the style and subject matter of the Codex Regius poems, and you end up with a significantly larger collection. Restrict yourself to the Codex Regius alone, and you lose material that clearly belongs with it. The edition you read will make choices about where to draw these lines. The choices are editorial, not natural.

What the corpus does have, regardless of where you draw the edges, is a shared sensibility. A way of looking at the world that is recognizable across poems, centuries, and manuscripts. Fate is real and inescapable. Knowledge costs something. Courage is not the absence of fear but the decision to act in its presence. The cosmos will end. Knowing that changes nothing about how you are required to live.

That sensibility is what this book is about. The manuscript history matters — it's the reason we have anything to read. The dating controversies matter — they tell us how the tradition evolved. But what matters most is the world that lives inside these poems. Taking it seriously. Letting it do what it was designed to do.

That work starts with the people who made it — and that's where we're going next.

Chapter 2
Skalds, Seers, and Anonymous Voices

Nobody signed these poems.

That fact is so basic it's easy to pass over, but stopping on it matters. In a literary tradition that placed enormous value on reputation — on the preservation of a name across time, on being remembered when you were gone — the poets of the Eddic corpus chose, or accepted, or were assigned, total anonymity. We don't know who composed the Völuspá. We don't know who first shaped the Völsung cycle into the form that reached the Codex Regius. We don't even know, in most cases, whether the poems as we have them represent a single poet's vision or the accumulated deposits of many voices over many generations. Anonymity is the default condition of this literature, and understanding why requires understanding what kind of poets made it — and what kind didn't.

Two Streams

Old Norse poetry divides, roughly and usefully, into two streams.

The first is skaldic poetry. Skalds were named poets — professional, court-based, technically extraordinary. They composed verse in meters of labyrinthine complexity, dense with kennings (the elaborate metaphorical compounds that substitute for simple nouns: the sea becomes the "wound of the whale," a battle becomes the "dew of shields"), governed by rules of syllable count and internal rhyme that make the strictest sonnet look improvisational. Skaldic verse was virtuosic by design. It was meant to be difficult — to advertise the poet's skill as clearly as the content advertised the patron's glory. We know skaldic poets by name: Egill Skallagrímsson, Snorri Sturluson himself, dozens of others. Their verses were preserved because their names gave the verses authority. A poem by Egill was valuable because Egill was a known quantity — a specific person with a specific life, whose testimony about a specific battle or king carried weight.

The Eddic poems are the other stream. They are anonymous, formulaic, and apparently impersonal — built from recurring phrases, standard epithets, shared narrative structures that could be learned and reproduced and modified without any single author claiming ownership. Where skaldic verse wears its difficulty as a badge, Eddic verse moves with a deceptive simplicity: short lines, strong rhythms, direct speech. Where the skald says I — this is my poem, these are my words, hear what I witnessed — the Eddic voice seems to come from everywhere and nowhere. It doesn't claim personal authority. It claims something older.

This distinction has a consequence that's easy to miss. Skaldic poetry was composed for specific audiences at specific moments — a king's victory, a jarl's funeral, a political alliance that needed celebrating. Its value was transactional, at least in part: the poet delivered praise, the patron delivered payment or prestige, the exchange was complete. Eddic poetry had no such transaction. It was composed for no single patron, no single occasion. It belonged to everyone who needed it and to no one in particular. That diffusion of ownership is what made it transmissible — and what made naming its author unnecessary. The anonymity is the record, not a gap in it.

The Custodial Poet

Custodial work is the most accurate description of what these poets did. The men and women who shaped and transmitted the Eddic corpus understood themselves not as creators but as keepers — vessels for material that predated them and would outlast them. This doesn't mean they were passive transcribers. Anyone who has studied oral tradition carefully knows that the "faithful transmission" model is a fantasy: every time a poem is performed, it changes, subtly or substantially, in response to the performer's skill, the audience's expectations, the occasion's demands. The Eddic poets were active shapers of their material. But they shaped it in the name of the tradition, not in their own name. The goal was not self-expression but preservation — keeping the old knowledge alive, in a form the living could use.

Where and when did that performance happen? The occasions varied. Some poems were almost certainly tied to ritual contexts — the blót, the seasonal sacrificial feast, where the community gathered to maintain its relationship with the divine world. Others belonged to funerary practice, recited at the graveside or the funeral pyre to send the dead off properly equipped with the right words. Others still were performed at secular gatherings — the long winter evenings in the hall, where entertainment and instruction were not yet considered separate categories. A poem like the Hávamál, with its practical wisdom about hospitality and caution and the management of friendship, would have been at home in almost any of these settings. A poem like the Völuspá, with its cosmic scope and ritual register, belonged somewhere more charged.

That custodial function is why the figure of the poet in this tradition looks so different from our modern assumptions about what a poet is. The Eddic poet is closer to a priest, or a librarian, or a specialist in memory than to the sensitive individual transforming private experience into art — someone whose personal identity is less important than the role she fills.

The Völva

Among all the figures who embody this role, one stands above the rest.

The völva — plural völur — was a seeress. A woman who practiced seiðr, a form of magic associated with prophecy, fate-working, and communication with the dead. The word is related to the verb sjá, to see — she is, literally, one who sees. In the historical record, völur appear as itinerant specialists, traveling between communities to perform their work for payment, called on particularly in times of crisis or uncertainty. They sat on raised platforms. They sang or chanted in a particular mode called varðlokur — spirit-locking songs — that was said to summon the spirits whose knowledge they then transmitted. They were respected, sometimes feared, occasionally reviled. They occupied a boundary position: powerful, necessary, and not quite safe.

The Völuspá — the most important poem in the corpus — is spoken entirely in the voice of a völva. Odin has called her up from death, or from the deep past, to tell him what she knows. She does, with the weary authority of someone who has seen everything and is unmoved by any of it. She tells him the creation of the world, the first war, the coming of Ragnarök, the death of the gods, the silence after, and the new world that rises from the sea when it's done. Then she descends again. The poem gives her no name. She doesn't need one. She is the voice that speaks what the gods themselves need to hear.

This is the highest function of the Eddic poet: to speak in the völva's register, from a position outside ordinary human time, transmitting knowledge that is larger than any individual consciousness. The voice is female for a reason. In the Norse cosmos, the boundary positions — the liminal spaces between worlds — were consistently occupied by women. Valkyries cross between the battlefield and Valhöll. The nornir sit at the root of the World Tree and weave fate. The völva moves between the living and the dead. These are the load-bearing roles in a system that can't hold without them.

The Problem of Writing

Oral performance was what these poems were designed for — to be carried in a human voice, in a specific space, before a specific audience, on a specific occasion. The rhythms of Eddic meter are not literary rhythms; they are mnemonic rhythms, built for memory and the mouth, with the alliteration and the strong stress patterns functioning as guide-rails for the performing poet. The formula — the repeated phrase, the stock description, the predictable structural unit — is not a sign of laziness. It's a technology. It gives the poet a toolkit, a set of ready-made components that can be assembled differently each time without requiring the performer to compose from nothing under pressure. It gives the audience something to hold onto, a familiar handhold in the flow of the performance.

When these poems were written down — sometime in the twelfth and thirteenth centuries, by Christian Icelandic scribes with good Latin educations and complex relationships to the material they were recording — something was gained and something was lost. What was gained is obvious: we have the texts. What was lost is harder to name. The performance context disappeared. The living voice was replaced by marks on vellum. The poem that had existed in its transmission — always slightly different, always responsive to the moment — was frozen into one version, one shape, one set of words.

The scribes who did this work were not neutral agents. They had reasons to preserve the poems — antiquarian interest, poetic education, cultural pride, the simple human desire to keep things from being forgotten — and they may have had reasons to modify them too. Christian concepts sometimes surface in poems that otherwise read as entirely pre-Christian. The Völuspá's description of a world reborn after Ragnarök has struck many readers as uncomfortably close to the Revelation of John. Whether this is because Norse and Christian thought independently arrived at similar visions, or because the scribe nudged the ending toward familiar theological territory, or because the poet who composed it was already working in a world partially shaped by Christian ideas — nobody can say for certain. The text we have is the text we have.

Reading the Poetic Edda requires a particular kind of critical humility. We are not reading the poems as they were performed in a ninth-century Norwegian hall. We are reading a thirteenth-century scribe's version of a tradition that had already passed through countless hands, voices, and cultural contexts before it reached parchment. That distance doesn't make the poems less powerful. It makes them stranger — layered with time in ways that add depth even as they complicate certainty.

What We Can Trust

The metrical structure, for one thing. Meter is conservative — it constrains what a scribe can change without destroying the poem, so the rhythmic architecture of the verse is likely to be close to the original. The core narratives, for another. Stories are resilient; they can survive transmission across centuries without losing their essential shape. What tends to shift in transmission is the surface — specific word choices, epithets, the occasional stanza that gets dropped or added — not the underlying skeleton.

What we can trust least is the frame. The introductory and concluding prose sections that appear around some of the poems in the Codex Regius — brief narrative contexts explaining who is speaking and why — are probably scribal additions, not part of the original poems. They're helpful for orientation and may preserve genuine traditions about how the poems were understood, but they're not the poems themselves. In a few cases, they actively flatten the ambiguity that makes a poem powerful, substituting a neat explanation for a productive uncertainty. Strip them away, and what remains is voice: unmediated, unframed, speaking from whatever time and place produced it.

That's the voice this book is trying to follow. Anonymous, custodial, often female, always older than it looks — the voice of people who understood themselves as keepers of something they hadn't made and couldn't own. They kept it well enough. It reached us.

The question now is what to do with it.

Chapter 3

The Oral Tradition

It is sometime in the tenth century. A poet stands in a hall — timber walls, fire at the center, smoke finding its way out through the roof. The audience is not silent the way a modern audience is silent. They shift, they drink, they know what's coming. The poem being performed tonight is not new. Everyone in the hall has heard a version of it before. That's not a problem. That's the point.

Novelty is not what anyone came for. What matters is the telling — the voice that carries the poem tonight, in this hall, for this occasion. Tomorrow night, in another hall, another poet will tell it differently. Some words will change. A stanza might move. A character might gain an epithet or lose one. The poem will still be the poem. Nobody will consider it corrupted. The idea that a poem has one correct, fixed form is a literary idea — a consequence of writing, of the ability to point at a page and say this, exactly this. Before writing, poems lived in their performance. They were events, not objects.

The Formula

The technical term for what makes oral poetry possible is formula — and it was the classicist Milman Parry who first identified it systematically, working on Homer in the 1920s before anyone had thought to apply the same framework to Norse verse. A formula is a fixed or semi-fixed phrase that fills a specific metrical slot: a noun-epithet combination, a line-unit, a small narrative block that can be inserted, modified, or combined with other formulas without breaking the meter or the sense. Parry's insight was that these formulas are not ornamental — they are structural. They are how oral poetry is made.

In Eddic verse, the formulas are everywhere once you learn to see them. Odin is consistently Alföðr — All-Father — in contexts that need a certain metrical weight. The sea is approached through a set of stock descriptions that vary by poem but draw from a shared pool. Moments of high emotion — the discovery of a betrayal, the approach of death, the utterance of a curse — tend to trigger recognizable structural patterns, almost like musical cues that signal to the audience what register they've entered. The poet is not copying these patterns mindlessly. The poet is deploying them, the way a jazz musician deploys familiar chord progressions — as a framework within which improvisation becomes possible rather than a constraint that eliminates it.

This is also why the audience's familiarity with the material is a resource, not a liability. When a Norse audience heard the opening lines of a poem they recognized, they didn't switch off. They leaned in. Familiarity creates anticipation — the pleasure of watching how this poet, tonight, navigates the known terrain. It also creates a kind of collaborative meaning-making: the audience brings everything they already know about a character or story to bear on what they're hearing, so the poem doesn't need to explain itself. It can move fast, cut deep, leave things unsaid. The Poetic Edda's famous compression — its ellipses, its gaps, its habit of skipping over what another tradition would labor to describe — is not obscurity but trust: the poet trusted the audience to fill in what was left out, and the audience was equipped to do it.

Occasions

The occasions that generated performance were varied, and the variation mattered. Not every poem belonged in every context.

The blót — the seasonal sacrificial feast that marked the major points of the Norse ritual calendar — was one setting. Here the poems that touched on cosmology, on the relationships between gods and humans, on the nature of fate, would have been most at home. The Völuspá, with its ritual frame of a seeress called up to speak to a god, reads like a text designed for charged occasions — its voice too large, too cosmic, for casual entertainment. The Grímnismál, with its systematic catalogue of divine dwellings and cosmic geography, has the quality of something recited in a context where the names of the gods and their domains needed to be spoken aloud and heard, as if the act of naming kept the world in order.

Funerary contexts generated their own poetry. The heroic laments — Guðrún weeping over Sigurðr's body, the elegies for the fallen — belong to a tradition of mourning poetry that was functionally integrated into the practice of grief. Speaking the right words at the right moment was not merely aesthetic. It was operational.

And then there were the secular occasions: the winter evenings in the hall, the gatherings that turned into informal competitions of storytelling and verse. The Hávamál's practical wisdom, the comic heroics of the Þrymskviða, the verbal sparring of the flyting poems — these are hall entertainment, designed to delight as much as instruct. Norse culture did not draw a sharp line between the sacred and the entertaining. Both required skill. Both required memory.

Memory as Technology

Without widespread literacy, memory is not a personal faculty. It is a social technology — distributed across a community, maintained by specialists, tested and refreshed through repeated performance. The poet who carries a tradition in their head carries a public obligation, not a private archive. When they die without having transmitted what they know, knowledge dies with them. This creates a specific relationship between the individual and the tradition: you don't own what you carry. You are responsible for it.

That responsibility carries particular weight in the Norse context, because what was being carried was not merely entertaining — it was cosmological. The poems of the Poetic Edda encoded a complete picture of the universe: its origins, its structure, its inhabitants, its eventual end. The names of the gods, the geography of the nine worlds, the order of events at Ragnarök — these were not trivial matters. They were the framework within which existence made sense. Losing them was not losing culture in the abstract. It was losing the map.

This is why the transmission continued long after the conversion to Christianity had made the material theologically inconvenient. The Icelandic scribes who wrote these poems down in the twelfth and thirteenth centuries were doing something the oral tradition had already been doing for centuries: deciding that this was worth keeping, regardless of what it cost. The decision to write it down was itself an act of memory — the last, most desperate form of it, chosen when the living chain of transmission was finally breaking.

The Paradox of Transcription

The paradox at the heart of the Poetic Edda is that transcription preserved the poems and falsified them simultaneously — preserved their words, falsified their nature. A poem composed for oral performance is a living event that happens to use words, not a fixed text that happens to be spoken aloud. Freezing it on parchment captures the words. It cannot capture the voice, the occasion, the audience, the specific quality of attention that a live performance generates, or the way a poem shifts meaning when performed for mourners rather than feasters, in a time of crisis rather than abundance.

What writing also cannot capture is the texture of variation — the accumulated differences between one performance and the next that, taken together, constitute the tradition's ongoing life. The Codex Regius gives us one version of each poem. In reality, each poem existed in as many versions as it had performances. The version the scribe wrote down was one snapshot of a moving target, and we have no way of knowing how representative it was of what most audiences heard most of the time.

None of this is reason to distrust what we have. It's reason to read it with the right kind of awareness — to understand that the text on the page is not the poem, but a trace of the poem, the way a fossil is a trace of the living animal. The shape is there. The weight and motion are gone.

What remains is still extraordinary. The compression, the power, the way certain lines land with a force that exceeds their apparent simplicity — these are the qualities that made these poems worth preserving in the first place. An oral tradition is ruthless: what doesn't work gets dropped, what works gets remembered. The Poetic Edda is, among other things, a record of what worked.

The tools those poems were built with are where we're going next.

Chapter 4

How to Read Old Norse Poetry

Open any translation of the Poetic Edda and something will feel immediately different — not foreign exactly, but slightly off-kilter, like a familiar room rearranged in the dark. The sentences are shorter than you expect. The images arrive without explanation. Things that seem like they should be connected are simply placed next to each other, the connection implied but never stated. And underneath all of it, if you read aloud, a pulse — a strong, irregular beat that doesn't match anything in contemporary poetry but feels, somehow, ancient in the most literal sense: as if it predates the conventions you grew up with and goes back to something more basic.

That feeling is accurate. Eddic poetry is built on principles that are genuinely older than most of what Western readers think of as poetic craft. Understanding those principles doesn't diminish the experience of reading — it deepens it. Once you know what you're listening for, the poems open up in ways that paraphrase and summary can't replicate.

There is a temptation, when approaching technically complex poetry from another culture, to absorb the content and ignore the form — to treat the myths as the point and the verse as merely a delivery mechanism. That temptation is worth resisting here, because in Eddic poetry the form is inseparable from the meaning. The meter tells you what kind of knowledge you're receiving. The kennings tell you how to see. The silences tell you what the culture considered too large or too true to be stated directly. Strip all of that away and you have the skeleton of something that was, in its original form, much more alive.

This chapter is a toolkit. Use it.

The Two Meters

The Poetic Edda has several meters, but two dominate the corpus and between them cover almost everything you'll encounter.

The first is fornyrðislag — "the measure of ancient words." It is the narrative meter, the one that carries story. Its basic unit is the long line, divided by a pause into two half-lines, each containing two stressed syllables. The lines are linked by alliteration — the stressed syllables in the first half-line must alliterate with the first stressed syllable of the second half-line. In performance, this creates a driving, forward momentum: the alliteration pulls the ear across the pause, and the regular stress pattern gives the verse a quality somewhere between speech and song. Fornyrðislag is the meter of the heroic poems, the narrative mythological poems, the poems that need to move. It has urgency built into its structure — even when the content is slow, the form pushes forward.

The second is ljóðaháttr — "the meter of songs" or "the chant meter." This one is stranger, and deliberately so. It alternates between pairs of long alliterating lines — the same principle as fornyrðislag — and single short lines that carry three stresses and stand alone, without a matching half-line. These short lines have a different feel entirely: more compressed, more oracular, as if the poem is stopping to breathe and what comes out in that pause is more concentrated than everything around it. Ljóðaháttr is the meter of the Hávamál, of the wisdom poetry, of the magical and ritual texts. It has a quality of incantation — something meant to be repeated, remembered, chanted rather than merely spoken. Where fornyrðislag carries you forward, ljóðaháttr periodically stops you. The short line drops like a weight.

Meter choice, in these poems, is never decorative. A poem in ljóðaháttr announces itself as belonging to a different register than a poem in fornyrðislag, the way a minor key announces something different from a major one. When the Hávamál shifts between practical wisdom and the account of Odin's sacrifice on the World Tree, it stays in ljóðaháttr throughout — but the meter does different work in each section, the same structure carrying radically different emotional freight. Learning to feel the difference between these two meters, even in translation, gives you a tool for understanding what a poem is doing before you've processed a single image.

In translation, the meters are inevitably softened or lost. But their ghost remains. Fornyrðislag poems in English tend to feel propulsive, declarative, clipped. Ljóðaháttr poems feel more halting, more weighted, as if each stanza needs to be absorbed before the next one arrives. If you find yourself slowing down involuntarily in the middle of a poem, you're probably in ljóðaháttr territory. That slowing is the meter doing its job, even across a thousand years and two languages.

Alliteration

In modern poetry, rhyme is the primary sound-binding device. In Eddic poetry, alliteration does that work — and it does it structurally, not ornamentally.

The difference matters. When a contemporary poet uses alliteration, it's typically for local effect: a phrase, a line, a moment of sonic emphasis. When an Eddic poet uses alliteration, it's the architecture. Every long line depends on it. The alliterating syllables are the load-bearing elements of the verse, the joints that hold the half-lines together. A line without proper alliteration is not a stylistic choice — it's a broken line.

Reading Eddic poetry in translation always involves a loss. The translators who try to reproduce the alliterative structure — Lee Hollander is the most committed to this in English — give you the closest approximation of how the verse actually worked, at the cost of sometimes torturing the word order. The translators who prioritize natural modern English — Jackson Crawford, Carolyne Larrington — give you cleaner prose but strip out the sonic architecture. Neither solution is wrong. Both involve sacrifice. Knowing what's been sacrificed helps you read what remains more accurately.

Even in translation, traces of the original pattern surface. The stressed words cluster. The important nouns and verbs carry the weight. The rhythm, however imperfectly reproduced, gestures toward what the original sounded like. Pay attention to those gestures.

Kennings

A kenning is a compound metaphorical phrase that substitutes for a simple noun — not a comparison (the sea is like a wound) but a substitution (the wound of the whale instead of the sea). The replacement is absolute: in a poem that uses the kenning, the simple noun may not appear at all.

The range of kennings in Old Norse poetry is enormous. The sea alone generates dozens: the whale-road, the fish's bath, the wound of islands, the eel-home. Gold is the fire of the river, the seed of the heath, the tears of Freyja. A sword is the wound-snake, the harm-rod of battle, the ice of blood. A warrior is the feeder of ravens, the reddener of shields, the tree of weapons. A woman is the linen-goddess, the birch of the drinking horn, the goddess of the necklace.

The kennings are not random. They draw on a shared system of mythological and natural knowledge — to understand the tears of Freyja as gold, you need to know the myth of Freyja weeping red gold for her absent husband Óðr. To understand the feeder of ravens as a warrior, you need the image of ravens feeding on battlefield dead. The kennings are compressed allusions, assuming an audience steeped in the same tradition the poet is drawing from.

Consider what happens when you encounter the kenning Yggdrasill's ash for the World Tree. On the surface it's circular — you're calling the tree by a name that already refers to the tree. But Yggdrasill itself is a kenning: it means, roughly, "Odin's horse," because the gallows on which Odin hanged himself is a kind of horse he rides between worlds. So the "ash of Odin's horse" encodes, in four syllables, the entire myth of the hanging, the nine days, the runes, the shamanic journey between worlds. An audience that knew the tradition heard all of that in the name. An audience that didn't heard nothing but a tree. The kenning rewards knowledge. It is inert without it.

Kennings restructure the act of reading. They force you to assemble meaning rather than receive it — to hold two images simultaneously and feel the meaning that lives in the gap between them. Reading poetry dense with kennings is an exercise in a particular kind of attention — lateral, associative, comfortable with the unresolved.

When you encounter a kenning you can't parse, it's usually because you're missing a piece of mythological background that the original audience had automatically. The appendix in this book is partly designed for exactly that problem.

The Eloquence of Silence

The Poetic Edda does not explain itself. This is not a failure of communication. It is a deliberate poetic strategy, and recognizing it as such changes how you read.

Modern narrative — whether prose or poetry — tends toward transparency. The connections between events are made explicit. The emotional states of characters are described or analyzed. The significance of an image is often stated directly, in case the reader misses it. The Eddic poems do none of these things. They present. They juxtapose. They stop.

In the Völuspá, the seeress describes the death of Baldr — the most beloved of the gods, killed by a mistletoe dart thrown by his blind brother Höðr, engineered by Loki — in a handful of lines, with no commentary on what it means, no authorial grief, no explanation of why this event signals the beginning of the end. The poem simply shows it and moves on. The weight of it accumulates in the silence around the lines, in what isn't said.

In the heroic poems, this technique reaches its extreme. The Atlakviða covers the destruction of the Nibelung dynasty — the killing of Gunnarr and Högni, the slaughter of Atli's children, the burning of the hall — in terse, accelerating stanzas that feel almost impatient with their own violence. There is no space for the reader to settle or mourn. The events happen, the poem moves forward, the silence after each stanza is where the horror lives.

The Hamðismál takes this even further. When Hamðir kills his brother Erpr in a moment of stupid rage — the brother who would have saved them all — the poem records the act and moves on in the same breath. No remorse, no reflection, no narrative pause to register what has been lost. The loss registers in the structure: the next time Hamðir and Sörli need a third man and don't have one, the reader feels

Erpr's absence as a physical gap in the verse. The poem manufactured that gap sixty lines earlier and said nothing about it. That is craft of a very high order.

This is the quality that makes the Poetic Edda feel genuinely archaic in a way that Snorri's prose does not. Snorri explains. He contextualizes, he moralizes, he occasionally editorializes. The Eddic poets trust silence to do the work that words can't. They compress not because they lack material but because they understand — with the confidence of people who know their audience will bring the rest — that what is left out can be more powerful than what is put in.

Reading with that understanding requires a different kind of patience. When a poem stops abruptly, when a character's motivation is never stated, when two scenes are placed next to each other with no connecting tissue — don't reach for a missing explanation. Sit with the juxtaposition. Let the gap do its work.

A Brief Glossary of Metrical Terms

For reference as you move through the chapters that follow.

Fornyrðislag — "the measure of ancient words." The primary narrative meter of the Eddic corpus. Long lines divided into two alliterating half-lines, each carrying two stressed syllables. Used in the heroic poems and the more narrative mythological poems.

Ljóðaháttr — "the chant meter" or "the meter of songs." Alternates between pairs of long alliterating lines and single short lines with three stresses. The meter of wisdom poetry, magical texts, and ritual verse. Produces an oracular, incantatory effect.

Málaháttr — "the meter of speeches." A variant of fornyrðislag with slightly longer half-lines and a heavier, more formal feel. Used occasionally in the heroic poems, particularly in dialogue-heavy sections.

Kenning — a compound metaphorical substitution for a simple noun. Draws on shared mythological and natural knowledge. Requires the reader to assemble meaning from two juxtaposed images.

Alliteration — the repetition of initial consonant sounds (or any vowel sounds) across the stressed syllables of a long line. The structural binding principle of Eddic verse, not an ornamental feature.

Stanza — the basic unit of Eddic verse organization. Typically four to eight lines, depending on meter. In the manuscripts, stanzas are marked but not visually separated the way modern poems are.

Heiti — a simple poetic synonym, less complex than a kenning. Where a kenning substitutes a metaphorical compound, a heiti substitutes a single alternative word — gjöll for "sound," hildur for "battle." Often archaic terms kept alive specifically in poetic contexts.

These are the instruments. The poems are the music. What follows, in the chapters ahead, is an attempt to hear what they were actually playing — and why, more than a thousand years after the last hall went quiet, it still carries.

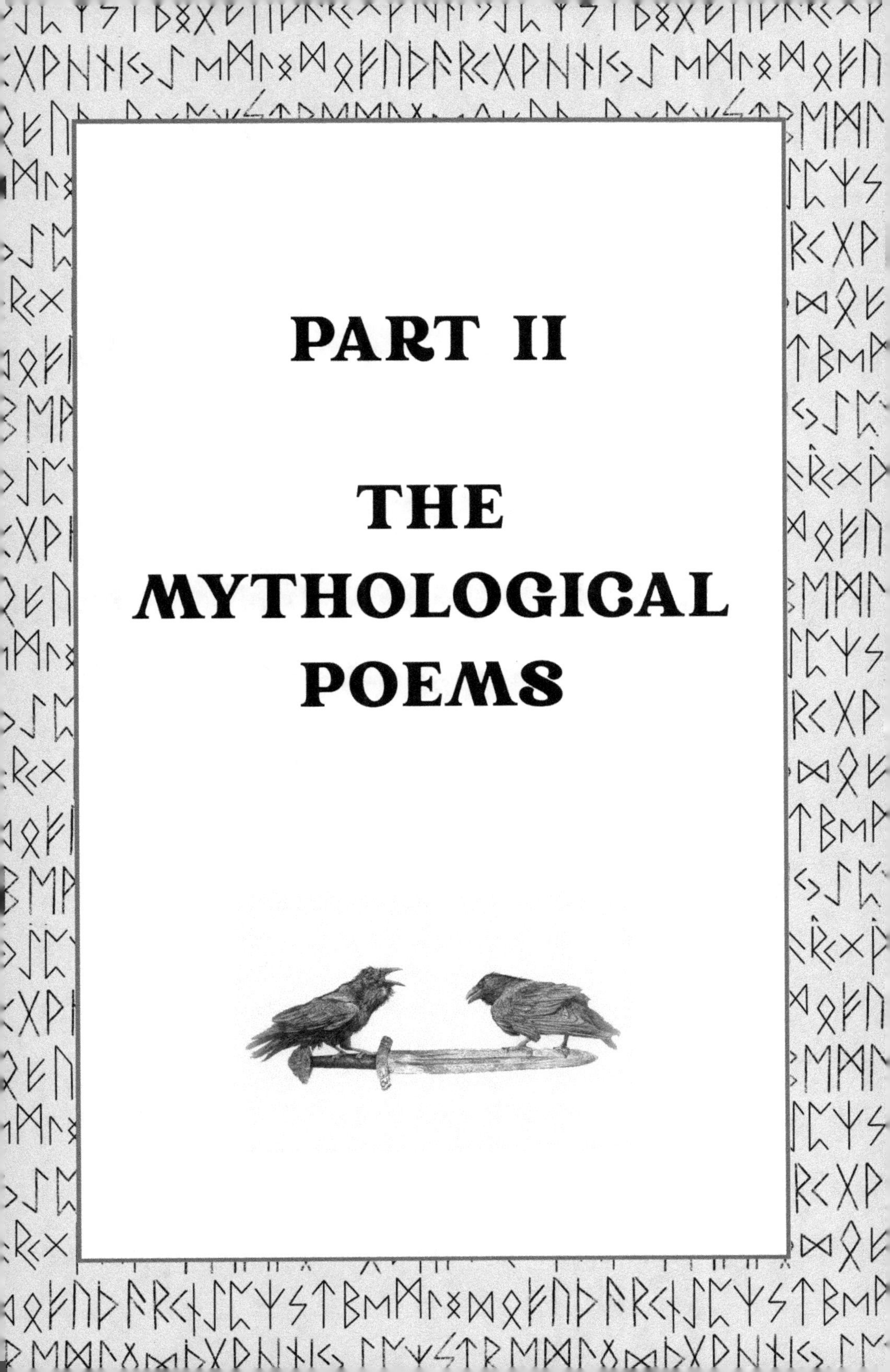

PART II

THE MYTHOLOGICAL POEMS

Chapter 5

Völuspá: The Seeress Speaks

She has been dead for a long time. That is the first thing to understand.

When Odin calls the völva up from the earth at the opening of the Völuspá, he is summoning something older than the current order of the world — a consciousness that predates the gods themselves, that watched the void before creation and will watch the silence after Ragnarök. She speaks because he compels her to. She is not grateful for the summons. She is not interested in his approval. She tells him everything he needs to know and everything he doesn't want to hear, and when she is finished she descends again, back into whatever she came from. The poem gives her the last word. It does not give her a name.

This is how the Poetic Edda begins. Not with a god's proclamation. Not with a hero's genealogy. With the voice of a dead woman who has seen the whole shape of time and is not impressed by any of it.

Everything that follows in the corpus flows from that opening gesture.

The Poem and Its Place

The Völuspá — "The Prophecy of the Seeress," or more literally "The Saying of the Völva" — is the first poem in the Codex Regius and almost certainly was placed there deliberately. The compiler who assembled the manuscript understood what he had: a poem that functions as a frame for everything else, a cosmological overture that establishes the terms on which all the other poems operate. Creation, catastrophe, renewal — the Völuspá maps the entire Norse universe in sixty-six stanzas with the economy of someone who has seen it all and doesn't need to show off.

It survives in two versions. The Codex Regius version is the primary text — sixty-six stanzas, in ljóðaháttr, the oracular chant meter examined in the previous chapter. The Hauksbók version, compiled in the early fourteenth century by the Icelandic scholar Haukr Erlendsson, preserves a slightly different text with a handful of additional stanzas and some significant variant readings. The relationship between these two versions is not simply a matter of one being more correct than the other — they represent two points in the life of a poem that was still moving, still being shaped by use, at the moment it was fixed in writing. We will return to the differences between them, because in several places those differences change the meaning of what you're reading.

The dating is contested, as it is for most of the corpus, but the Völuspá is generally placed somewhere in the late tenth or early eleventh century — possibly composed in Norway before the conversion, possibly in Iceland shortly after, when the Christian framework was new enough that a poet could still imagine speaking from outside it. What's certain is that it was composed by someone who knew the tradition with complete command, who could compress centuries of mythological material into a single prophetic voice without losing the thread, and who understood — with the confidence of great art — that the most important things do not need to be explained.

The Cosmogony: Before the World Was

Before existence has the idea of itself, the völva begins. Her first move is to demand silence — not from a human audience but, implicitly, from Odin himself, from the assembled gods, from whatever is listening. She is about to speak of things that predate speech. Then she reaches back past memory: "Ár var alda / þat er ekki var" — there was an age of ages when nothing was. No earth. No sea. No above, no below. No distinction of any kind. In Old Norse: Ginnungagap — the yawning gap, the primordial emptiness before existence had the idea of itself. The word ginnunga carries connotations of magic and illusion as well as emptiness. The void is charged with potential, heavy with what it does not yet contain.

Out of this void the earth rises — heaved up from the sea, the poem says, made green. The sons of Burr, Odin and his brothers, lift it into being. They make the sun and give it a course. They make the moon. They name the years, the seasons, the days. They build the divine residences. The act of creation in the Völuspá is not an act of speech, as in Genesis — God says and it is. It is an act of labor and naming: things are made, then given the names that fix them in existence. The distinction is subtle but important. The Norse cosmos is built, not spoken. It is a construction, and constructions can fail.

Walking on the land they have made, the gods find two trees: Ask and Embla, ash and elm, lying without breath, without sense, without heat, without color. Three gods give them what they lack. Odin gives önd — breath, the animating force, the same root as óðinn itself, the name of the god who breathes life into the first humans. Hœnir gives óðr — sense, consciousness, the inspired mental faculty that makes humans capable of poetry, prophecy, and frenzy in equal measure. Lóðurr — the third figure — gives blood and good color, the physical vitality that makes the body a home for the spirit that now inhabits it.

Who is Lóðurr? The tradition offers no certain answer, and the scholars who have pursued the question for the better part of two centuries have not resolved it. The leading candidate remains Loki, on the grounds that he is frequently Odin's companion in this kind of creative mythological adventure, that no independent figure named Lóðurr appears anywhere else in the corpus, and that the gift of blood and bodily life fits Loki's consistent association with physical matter, transformation, and the earthier dimensions of existence. The identification cannot be proven. But if it holds — if the trickster who will engineer the world's ending is also the one who gives humanity its body — the irony is perfectly Norse: the agent of destruction present at the moment of creation, his hands literally on the first human beings, the ending already folded into the beginning.

The Age of Gold and Its End

The gods build — halls, tools, divine residences — and then, in the poem's most quietly devastating gesture, they play hnefatafl in the grass outside. The poem calls this the age of gold, and its tone is unmistakably elegiac even as it describes something joyful: the golden age is narrated from its other side, by a voice that knows exactly how it ends. The happiness is real. So is its brevity.

The age ends with the arrival of three giant women from Jötunheimr. The poem doesn't explain their significance — it doesn't need to. Any Norse audience would recognize the nornir, the three weavers of fate who sit at the root of Yggdrasill and carve the destinies of gods and humans into the wood. Their arrival means that fate has entered the world. After them, the game in the grass stops. History begins.

What follows is the first war. The Æsir and the Vanir fight — the two divine families whose uneasy integration defines the Norse pantheon as the tradition knows it. The cause is Gullveig, a Vanir figure associated with gold and with seiðr magic, whom the Æsir burn three times. She rises each time, reborn. Her third resurrection gives her a new name: Heiðr, the honored one, the seeress who is welcomed in every hall. The Æsir's violence against her fails completely and permanently. This matters: the gods of war and sovereignty discover that the gods of fertility and magic cannot be destroyed by force. The Vanir power is of a different order — it absorbs violence and returns it transformed.

The war ends in truce, exchange of hostages, and integration. Njörðr, Freyr, and Freyja cross from the Vanir world into the Æsir world and stay. The pantheon that emerges — Odin and Thor standing alongside Freyr and Freyja — is a coalition with a violent founding, not a natural unity. It carries the memory of its own civil war. When Loki, centuries later in narrative time, stands up at the gods' banquet and begins to strip away their dignity one by one, he is working with material that was always there, just below the surface. The Völuspá plants the seed of Lokasenna in its first dozen stanzas.

The Presages: The Signs Before the End

The middle section of the Völuspá is a catalogue of omens, and its pacing is one of the poem's great achievements. Each sign is given as much space as it needs — no more — and the accumulation creates a pressure that builds stanza by stanza.

Baldr begins to have bad dreams. The gods hold council. Frigg extracts oaths from everything in existence not to harm him — every plant, every stone, every metal, every creature. Everything swears. Everything except the mistletoe, which she considers too young and small to matter. Loki finds the exception. He fashions a dart and guides the hand of the blind god Höðr. Baldr falls. The gods are silent.

That silence is the poem's most devastating effect. After the constant forward motion of the narrative — creation, war, building, betrayal — everything stops. The Völuspá gives this moment almost no space and then moves on. The restraint is the point. What cannot be adequately described is left to the silence around the stanza, which is where the grief lives.

Loki is found and bound in the earth with the entrails of his son Narfi, a serpent positioned to drip venom on his face. His wife Sigyn holds a bowl to catch the drops, but when she empties it the venom falls and Loki convulses — and when Loki convulses, the earth shakes. Norse audiences experiencing an earthquake knew what it meant: the god they had imprisoned was in agony, and the world was not large enough to absorb it quietly. This is myth functioning as geology, explanation woven so deeply into cosmology that the natural and the divine become the same thing.

Then the final roster of alarms. The cock Fjalarr crowing blood-red in the forest of Gallows Wood. The golden cock crowing in Valhöll. The rust-red cock crowing in Hel's domain below. Three worlds, three thresholds, three alarms in sequence from the highest to the lowest. The Norse cosmos is vertically structured — Ásgarðr above, Miðgarðr in the middle, Hel below — and the end-signal travels the full length of it, top to bottom, leaving nothing untouched. Fenrir's chains will break. Jörmungandr will rise. The ship Naglfar, its hull built from the uncut fingernails and toenails of the dead — which is why the Norse cut the nails of their corpses before burial, to slow its construction — will be launched. Each image arrives and departs in two or three lines. The poem trusts that you feel the weight without being told to feel it.

Ragnarök: The Accounting

Precision, not chaos, governs the apocalypse sequence. Every death was arranged long before it arrives.

Heimdallr raises the Gjallarhorn. Yggdrasill shudders through all its roots. The gods arm themselves. Odin rides to the well of Mímir to consult the severed head one final time — one last intelligence-gathering mission by the god who has spent his entire existence paying impossible prices for knowledge. Whatever Mímir tells him, the poem doesn't say. Then the battle begins.

The deaths are enumerated with the flat, implacable tone of a military report. Odin faces Fenrir and is swallowed. Víðarr avenges him — tearing the wolf's jaws apart, stepping on the lower jaw with a shoe that has been in construction since the beginning of time, assembled from the scraps of leather that cobblers trim from heels and toes, which is why Norse cobblers were careful to discard those scraps. Even the craftsmen of Miðgarðr, going about their daily work, were participants in the cosmological drama. Thor kills Jörmungandr and falls nine steps after the killing blow, poisoned. Nine steps: the sacred unit of distance in the Norse ritual world, the number of nights Odin hung on the tree, the number of worlds on Yggdrasill's branches. Thor makes it far enough to die with the serpent dead behind him. Freyr fights Surtr without his magic sword — the sword he surrendered for love of the giantess Gerðr, a transaction with consequences the Skírnismál traces in full — and falls. The cost of desire, paid at the end of everything, in full. Loki and Heimdallr kill each other simultaneously, two ancient enemies completing a transaction that the cosmos apparently required.

Surtr engulfs the earth in fire. The sea rises. The sky splits. The stars fall.

What makes this sequence devastating is not its violence but its geometry. Every death here was set up elsewhere — in other poems, in other stanzas of this poem, in the accumulated knowledge of an audience that knew the tradition. The Norse gods do not die in surprises. They die in fulfillments. Odin has known since before the poem began that Fenrir will swallow him. He has consulted every possible source of wisdom about it. He has sent his sons to avenge him, arranged for Víðarr to survive specifically for that purpose. None of it saves him, because none of it was meant to. The point was not to escape the death. The point was to meet it with everything in order, having done everything that could be done.

This is the ethical core of the Völuspá. Courage, here, is not the belief that you will win. It is the decision to act with full integrity in the face of certain loss — not because the outcome might change, but because who you are while facing it is the only thing that remains yours. The gods' heroism has nothing to do with power. It comes from knowing how they will die, and living as if that knowledge changes nothing about how they are required to behave. The Norse had a word for this quality — drengskapr — and the Völuspá is its highest expression in the corpus.

The Two Versions: Where They Differ

The differences between the Codex Regius and Hauksbók texts are concentrated in two areas, and both areas matter for interpretation.

The first concerns a stanza describing Náströnd — the shores of the dead — where the worst of the wicked are punished. The Hauksbók version gives this more emphasis, expanding the description of the hall and its inhabitants in ways that feel distinctly influenced by Christian concepts of hell: a place of calibrated punishment, full of oath-breakers and murderers wading through rivers of venom. The Codex Regius version is sparer. The difference suggests a scribe drawing on a slightly different source tradition, or shading the material toward theological expectations his audience would recognize. The Hauksbók Náströnd is a more Christian place than its Codex Regius counterpart. Knowing that changes how you read it.

The second difference is in the renewal sequence. The Hauksbók adds stanzas not found in the Codex Regius, including one that describes a powerful unnamed figure arriving from above. The identity of this figure has been argued over for generations. Some scholars read it as a surviving high god, possibly Odin in transformed form. Others read it as a direct Christian interpolation — a god of judgment inserted to resolve the theological discomfort of a cosmos that ends without anyone being held accountable. The Codex Regius is deliberately ambiguous on this point: something arrives, something oversees the new world, but the poem declines to name it. The Hauksbók makes it less ambiguous. Whether that clarification preserves an older reading the Codex Regius obscured, or represents a later addition the scribe felt the poem needed, cannot be answered with certainty. It should not be answered with false confidence.

What the comparison gives us is a window into the poem's life — evidence that it was being actively interpreted and adjusted even as it was being preserved. The Völuspá was a living text in the thirteenth century, caught in an ongoing argument about what the Norse cosmological tradition meant in a world that had become officially Christian. The disagreements are in the manuscript itself, for anyone willing to read both versions side by side.

Ragnarök and Revelation: Parallels and Divergences

The structural similarities between the Völuspá and the Book of Revelation are real enough that they cannot be dismissed as coincidence or independent development alone. Both texts are visionary prophecy delivered in the first person. Both describe the destruction of the current cosmic order through a sequence of escalating catastrophes. Both end with the emergence of a new, purified world. Both feature a final battle between cosmic order and cosmic chaos. Both include a hall of the blessed and a place of punishment for the wicked.

Three positions are defensible. The first is direct influence: the Norse poet knew the Christian apocalyptic tradition and worked in dialogue with it, consciously or not. Iceland's conversion was recent; Christian texts were circulating; a poet of sufficient sophistication would have encountered them. The second is typological similarity: both traditions are independently working through the same deep human problem — how does the world end, and what if anything follows — and arriving at structurally similar answers because those answers reflect something fundamental about how narrative handles finality. The third is syncretism: the poem as we have it is so thoroughly layered with pre-Christian material and Christian framing that separating them is no longer possible, or perhaps meaningful.

What is not defensible is the position that the renewal ending is simply and purely pre-Christian, uncontaminated by the theological environment in which it was written down. The evidence doesn't support it. Equally indefensible is the position that the poem is essentially Christian mythology in Norse dress. The mortal gods, the world that ends without final judgment of individual souls, the fatalist cosmology in which even the divine are subject to a destiny they did not choose — these are not Christian ideas. They are something genuinely other, sharing certain structural features while diverging on everything that matters most.

The Völuspá is a poem written at a threshold. It stands between two worlds and belongs fully to neither. That tension — two cosmologies cohabiting in the same poem, neither fully resolving into the other — is the source of its enduring force, and what makes it so resistant to a single clean interpretation.

The Völuspá Now

In contemporary Asatru practice, the Völuspá functions as the central ritual text — recited at blót, quoted in sumbel, used as the cosmological foundation for a living religious practice reconstructed from fragmentary sources. Its function is liturgical in the most literal sense: it does what the völva's original performance was designed to do, anchoring a community in a shared understanding of where the world came from and where it is going. Spoken aloud, to an audience, in a charged context, the orality it was built for is partly restored — and by all accounts it sounds, in those moments, like what it was always meant to be.

What strikes readers outside that context, encountering it for the first time, is usually something simpler and harder to name. The feeling of a voice that knows more than it is saying. The strange comfort of a worldview that makes no promises — that looks at the destruction of everything and refuses to flinch, refuses to console, refuses to pretend that the ending is anything other than what it is. And then, having refused all of that, offers a new green earth rising from the sea anyway.

Not as a reward. Not as a judgment. Just as what happens next.

The Völuspá does not tell you that things will be fine. It tells you the shape of things, all the way to the end, and then a little beyond. That turns out to be enough. It has been enough for a thousand years.

Chapter 6

Hávamál: The Words of the High One

The Hávamál is not a collection of Viking wisdom. It is a survival manual from a god who nearly didn't survive.

That distinction matters. The poem is frequently domesticated — quoted in motivational contexts, reduced to its most aphoristic lines, treated as a Norse version of Poor Richard's Almanac with better weather and worse table manners. The practical wisdom is real, and we will spend time with it. But reading the Hávamál only for its proverbs is like reading the Book of Job only for its patience. The surface is not the point. The point is what the surface is built on: a portrait of Odin as a figure who has paid, repeatedly and catastrophically, for everything he knows — and who has concluded that the paying was worth it, every time, without exception and without regret.

The poem is also, almost certainly, not a single poem.

A Composite Text

Scholars have identified at least five distinct sections within the Hávamál, each with its own tone, its own meter, its own apparent origin and function. The Gnomic Verses — the practical wisdom that opens the poem and constitutes its largest single section — read like accumulated communal knowledge, the kind of thing distilled from generations of hard experience and passed on without any single author's stamp. The Rúnatal — the account of Odin's self-sacrifice on Yggdrasill — has the compressed intensity of a ritual text, something designed to be spoken in a specific context with specific force, not read quietly but performed aloud in a charged setting. The Ljóðatal — the list of Odin's eighteen magical songs — reads like a catalogue, an inventory of power rather than a narrative, closer to a reference document than a poem in the ordinary sense. The Loddfáfnismál — a section of advice directed at a named recipient — has the feel of a separate wisdom poem absorbed into the larger collection at some point in its transmission history. And the episodes involving Odin's erotic adventures — his pursuit of Billingr's daughter, his seduction of the giantess Gunnlöðr — are narrative in a way none of the other sections are, closer to myth than to gnomic verse, closer to the Skírnismál or the Lokasenna than to anything else in this poem.

These sections were probably composed separately, over a considerable span of time, and brought together by a compiler who recognized that they all circled the same gravitational center: Odin as the archetype of the one who seeks knowledge at whatever cost. The compilation is not seamless. The joins are visible if you look for them, and the tonal shifts between sections can be jarring — moving from advice about when to leave a feast to a description of a god hanging in agony from a cosmic tree requires a certain flexibility in the reader. But the unity is real even if it is not organic. Each section contributes a different facet of the same portrait: the wise man in the world, the initiate at the threshold of death, the magician cataloguing his power, the teacher addressing his student, the trickster who loves what he destroys. The Hávamál is assembled from multiple angles, and the subject holds it together.

Reading it as a unified text, which this chapter does, requires accepting that unity without pretending the joins aren't there. The reward for that acceptance is a portrait of Odin — and through Odin, of a particular stance toward existence — that is more complete and more morally complex than anything else in the corpus.

The Gnomic Verses: How to Stay Alive

The poem opens with a man arriving at a door.

Before he enters, the Hávamál says, he should look around. He should look up and down, this way and that. He cannot know who is waiting inside, and caution costs nothing while carelessness can cost everything. This is not paranoia. It is the opening move of a poem that will spend its first section teaching a very specific kind of intelligence: not philosophical wisdom, not theological wisdom, but the practical alertness of someone who has learned, through damage, that the world is full of dangers that announce themselves quietly if at all.

The advice that follows covers an enormous range, and its quality varies — some of it is genuinely profound, some of it is the Norse equivalent of "look before you leap," and the poem makes no distinction between the two, which is itself a kind of wisdom. Hospitality comes first. A guest should not stay too long, because the welcome received on the first night is different from the welcome on the third, and a wise guest knows the difference before the host has to show it. Fire and food are the basics of human comfort — a person who has neither is already half dead in the body — and the host who provides them is performing something functionally sacred, where hospitality is not a courtesy but a moral obligation with cosmic weight.

Silence receives extended treatment. A fool who keeps his mouth shut can pass for wise indefinitely, while a fool who speaks removes all doubt. The poem is precise about why: the person who says little is giving nothing away, maintaining the informational advantage of the unknown, while the person who speaks without thinking is actively advertising his limitations to everyone listening. In this ethical world, where reputation is the only currency that matters, this is not a minor point. Words, once spoken, cannot be taken back. Every unnecessary word is a small surrender of position.

The treatment of alcohol is remarkable for a tradition so associated with mead-hall culture. The poem is not puritanical about drinking. It is unsentimental about the consequences of excess. The mead-hall is a central social institution and the Hávamál has no interest in dismantling it. But the man who cannot control himself in the hall is the man who will make enemies he doesn't remember making, break alliances he doesn't remember breaking, and wake up the next morning with a reputation he spent years building now quietly in ruins. The poem watched this happen. It is telling you not to be that man.

Friendship receives its most concentrated treatment here, and the Hávamál's conception of it differs so sharply from the modern one that it can seem cold until you understand what it is actually saying. The poem distinguishes between real friendship — which is reciprocal, which requires physical presence, which must be maintained through repeated contact or it dies — and the simulation of friendship, which costs nothing and delivers nothing. A friend at a distance, to whom you never go and never send gifts, is not a friend. He is a road you stopped walking. The relationship has not ended formally; it has simply become empty, and an empty relationship is worse than no relationship because it generates false expectations on both sides.

What the poem demands of friendship is mutual investment. You must show up. You must bring something. You must treat the friend's enemies as your enemies and the friend's difficulties as your difficulties, not because some abstract principle demands it but because that is what makes the relationship real. These are the ethics of a society where the individual without allies is the individual without protection, where the personal network is the only safety net that exists. In that context, friendship is not a luxury. It is infrastructure.

The ethical framework underlying all of this is entirely pre-Christian in its assumptions, and understanding it changes how you read the poem. There is no sin in the Hávamál — no offense against a divine law for which you will be judged in the afterlife, no original stain that needs washing, no transcendent authority keeping score. There is only reputation: what you are known to be among the people who know you. Dómr — the Norse word for judgment or renown — is the verdict of the community on your life and your death. Cattle die, the poem says. Kinsmen die. You yourself will die. What does not die is the renown of the one who dies well. This is not a consolation offered to make death easier. It is a challenge about what you are doing with the time you have. Who you are, you are in the eyes of others, and that is the only thing you will leave behind. The Hávamál's ethics belong to a culture that has no individual soul standing before God on judgment day — only a reputation that either survives in the mouths of those who outlive you or doesn't.

Some of the most psychologically acute material in the entire corpus appears in this section. The observation that a person who has been wronged should not let the wrong show until they are ready to act — that visible anger is wasted anger because it warns the enemy and gives him time to prepare — is the kind of thing that sounds like folk wisdom but operates at the level of strategic intelligence. The description of what it feels like to love someone who does not love you back — lying awake, running the same thought over and over, unable to find the exit — is so specific and so recognizable that it feels modern in a way that most ancient texts cannot manage. The Hávamál knows what it is to be inside a bad feeling and unable to get out. It does not offer comfort. It offers accuracy, which in the long run is more useful than comfort and harder to come by.

The Rúnatal: The Price of Knowing

Midway through the poem, without transition or warning, everything changes.

The gnomic voice — impersonal, communal, accumulative — gives way to the first person. Odin speaks directly. And what he says is this: he hung on the World Tree for nine nights, wounded by a spear, given to himself as a sacrifice, offered to himself by himself. No one gave him food. No one gave him drink. He looked down into the depths below the tree, seized the runes, fell back screaming into the world, and began to understand.

This passage — the Rúnatal, the account of the acquisition of the runes — is one of the most significant in the entire corpus. For those who have worked with the rune traditions, it is the foundational textual source for the central myth: the moment at which the runes enter the divine and human world, carried by the god who paid the full price for them. But the passage deserves close attention even outside that context, because it is doing something philosophically precise that goes beyond mythology.

Odin's sacrifice on Yggdrasill follows the structure of a shamanic initiation with a fidelity that is almost technical. Across cultures and centuries — from the Siberian shamanic tradition to the initiatory practices of West African religious systems to the mystery religions of the ancient Mediterranean — the initiatory pattern is consistent: the candidate undergoes a form of ritual death. Isolation, physical ordeal, symbolic or literal descent into the underworld. The initiate crosses a threshold that ordinary members of the community do not cross. And they return with knowledge or power that was unavailable before — a capacity for perception or action that exists on the other side of that specific kind of suffering. The death is not metaphorical. Something genuinely ends in the initiate, and what returns is constitutively different from what entered.

Odin on the tree is the god dying in order to become the god who knows what only the dead know. The runes he seizes at the bottom of his ordeal are not a writing system, though they can be written. They are the structure of reality as it becomes visible at the threshold between life and death — the patterns beneath the surface of things, the logic that governs cause and consequence at a level below ordinary perception. To acquire the runes is to acquire fluency in the language the cosmos is written in. Not the language of speech or narrative, but the language of deep structure, the grammar of how things actually work when you strip away the surface.

Nine nights: the sacred duration that appears throughout the corpus as the unit of ritual time. The wound from a spear: Odin's weapon, the instrument associated with sacrifice and with his own cult, here aimed at him by no one — or by himself, the poem says, in a formulation of extraordinary strangeness. Gefinn Óðni, sjálfr sjálfum mér — given to Odin, myself to myself. He is sacrificer and sacrifice simultaneously. The one who offers and the one who is offered are the same. The poem states it and moves on, because in the Norse understanding of sacrifice, this identity is the point, not the problem. The sacrifice acquires full power only when the distance between giver and gift is fully collapsed.

What the runes give him resists simple description, and the poem is wise enough not to attempt one. They are associated in the tradition with writing, with magic, with fate, with the deep architecture of the cosmos. They are carved on the roots of Yggdrasill by the nornir. They are spoken in healing charms and in curses. They are used in battle and in divination and in the turning of luck. To know the runes is to be able to read the structure of events below the level at which events announce themselves to ordinary consciousness. Odin on the tree is doing what the völva does when she prophesies — accessing a layer of reality that is normally obscured because ordinary waking consciousness is too full of its own noise to notice it. The difference is that the völva is summoned into that state by others. Odin drives himself into it, alone, through an act of self-administered violence.

The price he pays is absolute and described without drama. The suffering is not the point. The poem doesn't linger on the nine nights, doesn't describe the cold or the pain or the length of time. It names them and moves on, because the corpus is consistent about this: knowledge costs something real, it costs exactly as much as it is worth, and the transaction is concluded the moment the knowledge is obtained. Odin who gave his eye at Mímir's well, who sacrifices himself on the tree, who sends his ravens out each morning not knowing if they'll return, embodies a principle the entire corpus keeps returning to. There is no free wisdom. Every piece of genuine understanding you carry was paid for somewhere, by someone, in something that mattered. The only question the tradition asks is whether you are willing to pay.

The Loddfáfnismál and Gunnlöðr: Wisdom and Its Shadow

The Loddfáfnismál — the section of counsel addressed directly to the named figure Loddfáfnir — covers territory similar to the gnomic verses but in a more intimate register. The second-person address creates a different relationship: instead of wisdom broadcast into the air for whoever catches it, here is specific counsel given from a teacher to a student who has asked to be taught. The implication of a relationship, of a specific exchange, changes the emotional temperature. Some of the most concentrated ethical material in the poem appears here — the instruction not to wake before dawn to worry, because the night's half-light makes troubles appear larger than daylight will show them; the warning not to share your difficulties with a wicked person, because he will not use that knowledge to help you; the reminder that a man who steps beyond his competence and speaks beyond his knowledge will never know the moment he exposed himself, because no one will tell him.

Two narrative episodes involving Odin's erotic adventures appear between the Loddfáfnismál and the Rúnatal, feeling at first glance like interruptions of a different quality from everything around them. They are essential to the portrait.

The pursuit of Billingr's daughter is comedy, and Norse comedy has a specific quality — dry, precise, entirely unsentimental. Odin desires a woman. She apparently agrees to meet him, but when he arrives she is asleep, surrounded by guards, and he retreats. He waits. He comes back before dawn. The guards are gone. The woman has left a decoy in the bed — a dog tied to the bedpost where she was lying. Odin, who has made a career of outwitting every being in the nine worlds, has been outwitted by a woman with a dog and better timing than he had. The poem records his humiliation with the same flat tone it uses for everything else, and Odin concludes from the experience that the whole enterprise of pursuing an unwilling woman is a fool's errand. He is not wrong, and the fact that it took him this specific defeat to reach that conclusion is part of what makes the episode revealing.

Gunnlöðr's story is more complex and considerably darker. Odin seduces the giantess Gunnlöðr, daughter of the giant Suttungr, who guards the mead of poetry — the magical substance that confers the gift of eloquent verse on whoever drinks it. He drills into the mountain where she keeps it, spends three nights with her, and on each night she allows him a drink. He drinks all three vessels dry, transforms into an eagle, and flies back to Ásgarðr, where he vomits the mead into vessels that the gods then use to give the gift of poetry to worthy humans. Gunnlöðr is left behind. The oaths he swore to her — the poem implies he swore oaths — are broken.

Odin reflects on this with something between detachment and what might, in a different register, be recognized as guilt — he notes that he used Gunnlöðr ill, that what she got from him was not what she gave him. But he does not conclude that the theft was wrong. He concludes that the mead of poetry now enables human and divine verse, and that this was the necessary outcome. What the episode reveals about Odin is deliberate and not flattering: he lies, he seduces under false pretenses, he abandons a being who trusted him with something precious. The Hávamál includes all of this without softening it, because the portrait it is building is not morally simple and has no interest in pretending to be.

Placed alongside the Rúnatal, the Gunnlöðr story confirms the same principle from a different angle: the knowledge that matters most — the runes, the mead of poetry, the wisdom that gives access to the deep structure of things — cannot always be obtained by honest or comfortable means. Odin does what is necessary and he knows the cost. The poem lets you sit with that. It does not tell you how to feel about it, because how you feel about it is your problem, not the poem's.

The Ljóðatal: The Eighteen Songs

The final major section of the Hávamál is a list. Odin enumerates eighteen magical songs — incantations, formulas — describing the effect of each without revealing the words. This is the catalogue as art form: not giving the reader the thing itself but telling them what the thing does, which generates a specific effect somewhere between instruction and deliberate withholding.

The songs cover an enormous range of application. One blunts the edge of an enemy's sword before battle. One frees the bound from their chains — the poem is precise: the fetters spring from the feet, the bonds fall from the hands — specific enough to suggest actual ritual practice rather than literary invention. One stops an arrow in flight. One calms a storm at sea. One allows Odin to converse with the hanged — the executed dead, who were specifically his dead, sacrificed to him on the gallows that mirrors in the human world the World Tree on which he himself hung. Several songs involve reversal and healing: lifting curses placed by others, neutralizing poison, turning hostile magic back on its source.

The progression from song to song is not random. It moves from the physical — combat, binding, weather — through the psychological and relational, toward the increasingly esoteric: songs that control the minds of enemies, songs that reconcile the estranged, songs that work on the dead as well as the living. The catalogue enacts a kind of cosmological survey of the domains over which magical knowledge operates, which is to say all of them.

The eighteenth song — the last and most powerful — Odin will not reveal even in this context. He will tell it only to a woman lying in his arms, or to his sister. The poem closes on this withholding. After hundreds of lines of sharing what he knows, the last move Odin makes is to demonstrate the limit of what can be transmitted in verse or speech or public performance. The deepest knowledge is not for everyone. It does not pass through books or lectures or catalogues. It passes only in the most intimate possible context, between two people at the closest possible distance. Some things remain personal. Some things remain secret. Even a poem about a god who has paid everything for knowledge ends by insisting that there is something knowledge cannot be.

The Philosophy of the Hávamál

Reading the Hávamál as a unified text — holding its composite sections together as a portrait of a single intelligence — reveals a coherent philosophical position that has no precise parallel in either the Christian tradition or the classical one, though it has family resemblances to both and is finally reducible to neither.

The closest Western analog is Stoicism. The Hávamál's insistence on what is within your control — your reputation, your response to circumstance, your willingness to pay the cost of real knowledge — and its systematic indifference to what falls outside that circle mirrors the Stoic distinction between what is eph' hēmin — up to us — and what is not. The focus on maintaining composure and integrity under pressure, on being fully what you are regardless of what the world does to you, is recognizably the same project Marcus Aurelius is working on in his Meditations and Epictetus in his Enchiridion. The insistence that wisdom costs something real, that no genuine understanding is obtained without sacrifice, runs from Socrates through the Stoics with the same consistency it runs through Odin's entire mythology.

But the differences are as significant as the similarities, and they define what is distinctively Norse about the Hávamál's position. The Stoics locate virtue in conformity with a rational cosmic order — the logos, the divine reason that governs the universe and guarantees that right action is ultimately coherent with how things actually are. The Hávamál operates in a cosmos with no such guarantee. There is fate — örlög, the deep pattern woven before the gods were born — but fate is not rational in the Stoic sense, and it is certainly not good. It is simply what happens. Dómr — the reputation that survives you — is not a cosmic reward for right conduct. It is a human artifact, maintained in human memory, with no divine enforcement behind it. Good people die badly in this tradition, and the poem knows it. What the Hávamál offers is not the Stoic assurance that the universe is on the side of virtue. It offers something harder and, in its way, more honest: the argument that how you conduct yourself matters regardless of whether the universe notices.

The Hávamál is also more pragmatic than Stoicism in ways that can feel jarring to readers who come to it from a philosophical tradition that takes virtue as its own reward. The poem is interested in effectiveness — in being the kind of person who survives, who maintains useful alliances, who reads situations correctly and acts accordingly. The ethical person of the Hávamál is a skilled navigator of a difficult world — someone who has internalized enough hard-won knowledge to move through life without losing what matters to them. Virtue is a by-product of that navigation, not the declared goal. The wisdom is practical before it is philosophical, and it earns its philosophical weight through the accumulation of practical detail rather than by asserting it up front.

This is why the Hávamál remains the most immediately readable poem in the corpus for contemporary audiences — more readable, in some ways, than the Völuspá or the Völsung cycle, whose power depends heavily on engagement with the mythology. The concerns of the gnomic verses are permanent concerns: how to make friendships that last, how to know when you're being deceived, how much to say and when to stay silent, how to maintain your sense of self when circumstances push hard against it. The poem's answers are specific enough to feel earned and general enough to apply to situations its composer never imagined. That combination — specific wisdom with general application, stated without apology and without the promise of any reward for following it — is what the Hávamál offers its reader.

It makes no promises. It does not tell you that following its counsel will make things go well. It tells you that following its counsel will make you the kind of person who faces what comes with the best possible preparation, the clearest possible eyes, and the most durable possible sense of who you are. What comes after that is not the poem's business.

That's yours.

Chapter 7

Vafþrúðnismál: The Wisest of Giants

There is only one way to win a wisdom contest with Odin. You have to already be Odin.

The Vafþrúðnismál — "The Sayings of Vafþrúðnir" — is built around this paradox, and it exploits it with the controlled precision of a trap being set in plain sight. Odin travels to the hall of the giant Vafþrúðnir, the wisest of all the frost giants, and challenges him to a flyting: a contest of knowledge in which each party asks a question the other must answer correctly, and the one who cannot answer loses his head. The stakes are stated at the beginning and never varied. This is not a metaphor. The loser dies.

What the reader knows, and the giant doesn't, is that the traveler calling himself Gagnráðr — "the one who gives good counsel," a name so transparently an Odin alias that it barely qualifies as a disguise — is the god who sacrificed his eye for wisdom at Mímir's well, who hangs on the World Tree for nine nights to win the runes, who sends his ravens out every morning to gather intelligence about everything that moves in the nine worlds. Vafþrúðnir is genuinely wise. He just isn't that wise. And the poem, which knows this from the first stanza, takes its time letting him find out.

The Format: Flyting as Cosmology

The flyting — the ritual contest of insults, boasts, or knowledge — is a recurring structure in the Eddic corpus, and it deserves attention as a form before we enter this particular example. The flyting is not merely competitive entertainment. It is a technology for transmitting information in a context that demands it be accurate. In a wisdom contest where the stakes are fatal, no one bluffs. Every answer must be correct, because an incorrect answer is not just a loss — it is exposure. The flyting strips away the possibility of vagueness and forces the contestant to commit to precise knowledge or die on the ambiguity.

This makes the flyting an efficient vehicle for cosmological instruction. Vafþrúðnir knows the Norse universe in its full technical depth — the names of the horses that pull the sun and moon across the sky, the rivers that mark the boundary between the worlds, the fates of individual gods at Ragnarök, the nature of existence before creation. As the contest progresses and each question demands a more comprehensive answer, the poem delivers a systematic survey of Norse cosmological knowledge without ever feeling like a lecture. The dramatic frame earns every piece of information it transmits. You need to know what Vafþrúðnir knows, because if he doesn't know it he dies.

The ljóðaháttr meter reinforces this quality. The short, weighted lines that characterize the chant meter give each answer a finality — a sense of something being stated that will not be revised or qualified. When Vafþrúðnir speaks, the universe he describes feels fixed, authoritative, the product of knowledge that has been carried for a very long time. He is reporting, not speculating.

The Questions and What They Reveal

Both sides open cautiously, feeling out the terrain before committing to it. Odin, presenting himself as a wanderer who has come seeking wisdom, asks to be tested before he sits at the giant's table — a piece of formal courtesy that is also a chess move, because it forces Vafþrúðnir to engage before he has assessed his opponent. The giant accepts, and the early questions are almost administrative: the names of the horse that draws day across the sky, the horse that draws night, the river that divides the worlds of gods and giants. These are foundational questions, the cosmological equivalent of asking someone to name the planets before moving to orbital mechanics. Vafþrúðnir answers them correctly and easily, because the poem needs to establish his credentials before it can make the ending mean anything.

Then the questions deepen. Where does winter come from? The giant Vindsvalr, who is cold and merciless — his disposition is the season. Where does summer come from? From Svásuðr, whose name means something like "the pleasant one." The Norse cosmos is not impersonal. Its weather has parents, its days have names, its rivers are beings with histories. This is the quality that makes Norse cosmology feel different from a cosmological diagram — it is a world in which everything that exists has a genealogy, a story, a relationship to everything else. The questions pull that world into view one thread at a time.

The answers become more technical and more esoteric as the contest progresses. Vafþrúðnir names the primordial giant Aurgelmir — who precedes Ymir in the genealogy of the frost giants, the giant before the giant from whose body the world was made — and describes his origin in the venomous rivers of Élivágar, before the separation of fire and ice had produced anything recognizable as life. He describes Bergelmir, the giant who survived the flood of Ymir's blood when Odin and his brothers killed the primal giant and the blood drowned all the other frost giants — a story with obvious structural parallels to the Biblical flood, though the moral weight is distributed very differently. Here the flood is not a punishment for wickedness. It is a byproduct of cosmogony, the blood of the primordial body becoming the sea that fills the new world.

The questions turn toward eschatology. What will happen to the sun when Fenrir swallows it? The sun will have a daughter first, the poem says, and that daughter will ride her mother's paths after Ragnarök — the world's light will survive its own destruction through its own offspring. This is one of several places where the Vafþrúðnismál supplements and refines what the Völuspá tells us, filling in details that the older poem either skips over or handles too quickly for clarity. The two poems exist in productive dialogue: the Völuspá provides the broad frame, the Vafþrúðnismál populates it with specifics.

Where will the surviving gods go after Ragnarök? Vafþrúðnir names them: Víðarr and Váli will survive, unpoisoned by Surtr's fire and the sea's flood. Móðr and Magni will carry Thor's hammer. Baldr and Höðr will return from Hel, reconciled, and together they will rule the new world. Hœnir, obscure and rarely discussed in the tradition, will hold the sacrificial twigs — a detail that implies the continuation of ritual practice in the renewed world, which is among the more extraordinary things the corpus mentions without stopping to examine. The world after Ragnarök is not godless or religionless. It is a world that has been through the end of everything and resumed.

Odin's Turn: The Questions That Cannot Be Answered

When Odin begins to ask, the contest changes register entirely. Up to this point Vafþrúðnir has been asking his questions first, testing the stranger before agreeing to answer in kind. Odin has responded to each correctly and efficiently, giving nothing away, maintaining his disguise through a combination of accurate knowledge and careful deflection. He is not showing off. He is creating the impression of a very wise mortal — wise enough to have earned a seat at the giant's table, not so obviously omniscient as to reveal who he is.

Then Odin asks. And his questions go further than anything Vafþrúðnir has attempted — further than cosmological inventory, further than genealogy and eschatology, into the territory of things that should be unknowable. What did Odin whisper into the ear of Baldr when Baldr lay on his funeral pyre?

The question is unanswerable. Not because the answer is difficult to find or obscure in the tradition, but because there is only one being in the universe who could possibly know what was said in that moment: Odin himself. The poem has been building to this point since its opening lines. The flyting, the established format in which correct knowledge keeps you alive, has been inverted — now the correct knowledge is the knowledge that you have been deceived, that the being sitting across from you is not a mortal wanderer at all, and that you have already lost.

Vafþrúðnir understands immediately. His response is one of the great moments of acknowledgment in the corpus: he names Odin directly, without bitterness or self-pity, and concedes that he has been a fool to compete with the one who knows everything there is to know. He accepts his death. The poem ends without describing it — it doesn't need to. The giant has already been defeated by the question. What follows is a formality.

Deception as Epistemology

The ending illuminates something that runs through the entire Odin mythology and distinguishes it sharply from the divine figures of other traditions. Odin does not compete honestly. He never has. His disguises — Gagnráðr here, Vegtamr in the Baldrs draumar, Grimnir in the Grímnismál, the wandering old man with the broad-brimmed hat who appears throughout the sagas — are not occasional tactical choices. They are constitutive of who he is. The god of wisdom is also the god of masks. The knowledge he accumulates cannot be separated from the methods he uses to obtain it.

This is a consistent and deliberate feature of this theological vision, not a moral lapse that the tradition is embarrassed about. Where the Abrahamic traditions insist on a god who is essentially transparent — who says what he means, who requires the same honesty from his worshippers that he embodies himself — the Norse cosmos is entirely comfortable with a supreme divine figure who lies, disguises himself, manipulates his opponents, and wins through deception as readily as through strength or superior knowledge. The Vafþrúðnismál treats Odin's victory as fully legitimate. There is no suggestion that he should have competed fairly. The giant knew the stakes. He should have known his opponent better.

What makes this philosophically interesting rather than merely morally troubling is the implication that deception and wisdom are not opposites but partners. The being who is wise enough to know everything is also wise enough to know when to conceal what he knows — and how to use that concealment strategically. Odin's disguises are a form of intelligence: he learns by going incognito, by sitting in halls where people speak freely because they don't know who is listening, by asking questions that only a mortal would need to ask. The disguise is not a lie about who he is. It is a tool for finding out what the world looks like from a position other than his own.

The question about Baldr's funeral is the final expression of this principle. Odin wins not by knowing the answer but by knowing the question — by understanding that there exists a question that only he can answer, and that asking it in this context is the equivalent of checkmate. Knowledge, in the Vafþrúðnismál, is not merely what you possess. It is understanding what you possess that no one else does, and knowing when to reveal it.

The Vafþrúðnismál and the Völuspá: A Dialogue

Reading the two poems together reveals a relationship that is almost collaborative. The Völuspá is expansive, prophetic, emotionally weighted — it gives you the shape of the Norse universe at the level of feeling. Technical, additive where the Völuspá is prophetic and felt, the Vafþrúðnismál gives you the same universe at the level of inventory. Where the Völuspá describes Ragnarök in a sustained vision of escalating catastrophe, the Vafþrúðnismál answers specific questions about what happens on the other side of it: which gods survive, what they carry with them, what the world looks like when it reassembles itself.

What each poem emphasizes is itself informative. The Völuspá focuses heavily on Baldr's death and Loki's imprisonment as the triggers for Ragnarök — the moral failures within the divine community that set the end in motion. The Vafþrúðnismál is less interested in moral causation and more interested in mechanical structure: the fates of individual gods, the genealogies of cosmic forces, the precise sequence of events from the breaking of Fenrir's chains to the emergence of the new earth. Together they constitute something close to a complete Norse cosmological system — one providing the prophecy, the other the technical manual.

Whoever compiled the Codex Regius almost certainly understood this complementarity when placing the Vafþrúðnismál immediately after the Völuspá. The reader who has absorbed the Völuspá's vision of the world's end arrives at the Vafþrúðnismál with questions the second poem is positioned to answer. Why does Freyr die without his sword? The Skírnismál will explain, but the Vafþrúðnismál confirms the fact. What happens after the fire? The giant's enumeration of the survivors fills in what the Völuspá's final stanzas leave deliberately ambiguous. The Codex Regius is a curated reading experience, and the curation is intelligent.

The Giant as Worthy Opponent

One last thing deserves attention before we leave this poem, and it is easy to miss if you read the ending too quickly.

Vafþrúðnir is a scholar — not a monster or a figure of evil, not the kind of antagonist a mythology hostile to giants would produce. He is a being who has lived long enough and thought carefully enough to accumulate the deepest knowledge of the cosmos available to any creature that is not Odin himself. He receives Odin with hospitality. He accepts the contest's terms without complaint. He answers every question correctly and honestly. And when he loses — when he realizes he has been deceived and that the disguised god sitting across from him has been Odin all along — he concedes with dignity and without self-pity.

That dignity matters. The Vafþrúðnismál is a poem about the nature of knowledge and its limits, and the giant embodies those limits with something close to nobility. He knew everything that could be known short of omniscience. He simply didn't know enough. In this cosmology, that is not a moral failure. It is a condition of existence. Even the wisest being short of Odin operates with incomplete information, and incomplete information, in a universe where the stakes are always ultimate, is eventually fatal.

The poem knows this. It respects the giant enough to let him understand what happened to him, and to leave him his last words. In a literature sometimes accused of celebrating brute force at the expense of everything else, the Vafþrúðnismál is a quiet reminder that the Norse valued intelligence above almost everything — and that the intelligence they valued most was the kind that knows what it doesn't know.

Chapter 8

Grímnismál: The Lay of the Masked One

Eight days he has been sitting between two fires, without food, without water, his wrists bound and the flames close enough to burn. This is his punishment from King Geirröðr, who was told by his wife that the stranger he'd captured was no ordinary wanderer and who, rather than release him or kill him cleanly, decided on prolonged torment as the appropriate response to divine trespass. It is not a wise decision. The king doesn't know yet that the bound man between his fires is Odin — Grímnir, the masked one, the hooded stranger who gives this poem its name — and by the time he finds out, it will be too late to do anything useful with the information.

This is the frame of the Grímnismál. It is a thin frame, almost perfunctory — the narrative setup is disposed of quickly and the narrative resolution even more quickly. What fills the space between them is the reason the poem exists: forty-four stanzas of pure cosmological inventory, a systematic mapping of the Norse universe delivered by a god in extremis, speaking apparently to no one, or to the young man Agnarr who brings him a drink of water on the eighth day and thereby earns everything that follows.

The Catalogue as Form

The Grímnismál is the most explicitly catalogue-like poem in the corpus — more so even than the Vafþrúðnismál, whose question-and-answer format creates at least the illusion of narrative movement. Here Odin simply speaks. He names the dwellings of the gods, one by one. He describes the path of the sun. He maps the World Tree with its tenants and its roots. He lists the rivers that flow from Hvergelmir, the great spring at the root of everything. He enumerates the Einherjar in Valhöll, the valkyries, the horses the gods ride to council. He recites his own names — a long list, one of the longest self-enumerations in the tradition — and in that list reveals himself to the king who is finally paying attention when it is already too late.

The catalogue as a poetic form has a bad reputation in modern reading culture, where it tends to signal padding or archaic convention. In this tradition it signals authority. The being who can name everything in a domain controls that domain, at least in the magical and cognitive sense that matters most here. The Grímnismál's lists are not inventory for their own sake. They are a demonstration of omniscience — a god proving, through the sheer exhaustive accuracy of his knowledge, who he is before he announces it directly. When Odin finally names himself at the poem's end, the revelation has already been enacted through the preceding forty stanzas. The name is just the confirmation.

Reading the Grímnismál requires accepting this logic — the catalogue must be received as what it is, not translated into narrative or read as if it were building toward a conventional dramatic climax. The pleasure of the poem is the pleasure of a complete picture assembling itself piece by piece: each dwelling named, each river listed, each inhabitant of Yggdrasill located in its proper place, until the Norse universe is present in the room in its full, articulated form.

The Dwellings of the Gods

Odin begins with the divine residences, and the list he produces is the most complete topography of Ásgarðr available in any single source.

Þrúðheimr belongs to Thor — the realm of power, where the thunder god lives with his hammer and his goats and his vast, uncomplicated appetite for combat and food. Ýdalir, the valley of yew trees, belongs to Ullr, the archer god whose profile elsewhere in the tradition is surprisingly low given that he once held Odin's place while the chief god was exiled. Válaskjálf is Odin's silver-roofed hall, from whose high seat Hliðskjálf he can see across all nine worlds simultaneously. Sökkvabekkr — the sunken benches — is where Sága and Odin drink daily from gold cups as cool waves wash over them, a scene of divine companionship whose precise mythological significance is never explained and perhaps doesn't need to be. Glaðsheimr, the bright world, is the sacred space where the twelve gods sit in counsel. Þrymheimr, the thunder-home in the mountains, belongs to the giant Þjazi, and after him to his daughter Skaði who chose it over the soft coastal hall of her husband Njörðr. Breiðablik — the broad gleaming — belongs to Baldr, and is described as the place where the fewest evil things are known: even his dwelling is defined by the absence of malice, as if the light that surrounds him repels darkness as a physical property.

What the list creates is a cosmological city, a map of divine habitation that makes the Norse divine world feel simultaneously vast and intimate. These are places with specific qualities, specific relationships to their inhabitants, specific histories embedded in their names — not abstractions, but addresses. Reading through them produces the feeling of being oriented — of knowing where you are in a universe that, without this map, would be a formless expanse of myth.

The Grímnismál's divine geography supplements the Völuspá significantly. Where the Völuspá gestures at the divine world as context for its cosmic drama, the Grímnismál makes it concrete and habitable. The two poems operate at different scales of resolution: one gives you the shape of the universe, the other gives you the addresses. Together they produce a more complete picture than either could alone, and the compiler of the Codex Regius, by placing them in close sequence, was clearly aware of this.

Snorri's Prose Edda draws heavily on the Grímnismál for exactly this material — the divine residences, the World Tree's inhabitants, the rivers of Hvergelmir. But as always, Snorri smooths and systematizes what the poem leaves rough. The Grímnismál's version of Ásgarðr is less tidy than Snorri's, its list less perfectly organized, its internal logic less apparently rational. This roughness is evidence of age — of a tradition that accreted over time without a single architect imposing order on it, a divine world that grew the way cities grow rather than the way blueprints are executed.

Yggdrasill: The World Tree in Detail

The Grímnismál's description of Yggdrasill is the most detailed in the corpus, and it repays slow reading.

Three roots support the tree. One reaches toward the Æsir — toward the divine world, where the nornir sit at the well of Urðr and water the tree daily from the sacred spring. One reaches toward the frost giants — toward Jötunheimr, where Mímir's well lies and where Odin paid his eye for a drink. The third reaches into Niflheim, the world of mist and cold, where it hangs over Hvergelmir, the spring from which all rivers flow and from whose vicinity the serpent Níðhöggr gnaws at the root from below.

Each inhabitant is located with the same precision. The eagle — unnamed here, as in most sources — sits at the crown, and between his eyes sits the hawk Veðrfölnir, the weather-pale one. The squirrel Ratatoskr runs up and down the trunk carrying messages between the eagle at the top and Níðhöggr at the bottom — messages that the poem implies are hostile in nature, designed to keep them in permanent antagonism. Four stags wander among Yggdrasill's branches eating the new growth: Dáinn, Dvalinn, Duneyrr, Duraþrór. Their names are cryptic and largely untranslatable, carrying suggestions of sleep and of something obscure moving in the depths. More serpents than can be counted lie coiled among the roots.

Yggdrasill is not a symbol in the literary sense, a vehicle for abstract meaning — it is a model, a structural diagram of how the Norse universe actually works: different worlds connected by a single living axis, in permanent tension between growth and decay, the creatures at its extremities unable to meet directly and therefore communicating through an intermediary who has a stake in keeping the conflict going. Ratatoskr is the world's first troll, in the internet sense — an agent of discord whose function is to ensure that the eagle and the serpent never run out of reasons to hate each other.

The waters of Yggdrasill are sacred. The nornir take water from Urðr's well every day and mix it with the white clay around the well's edge to pour over the tree's branches — keeping it green, keeping it alive, performing the daily maintenance that holds the cosmos together. Without this ritual act, the poem implies, the tree would wither. The cosmos requires tending. The universe is not self-sustaining. It persists because specific beings perform specific acts of care on a daily basis, and this is considered neither unusual nor heroic — it is simply the work that keeps existence operational.

The Rivers and the Hvergelmir

Running from Hvergelmir are rivers whose names constitute among the poem's most purely incantatory passages — a sequence of Old Norse words whose sounds carry more weight than their meanings, most of which are obscure even to specialists. Svöl, Gunnþrá, Fjörm, Fimbulþul, Slíðr, Hríð, Sylgr, Ylgr, Víð, Leiptr, Gjöll — the names accumulate into a sonic landscape, a river-world that exists in the ear as much as in the geography of the Norse cosmos.

The Grímnismál is the primary source for most of these names, and this is significant: the tradition treated naming as a form of preservation. To name all the rivers of Hvergelmir in verse was to ensure they were remembered — to make their existence a matter of poetic record that could be transmitted orally and would survive as long as the verse survived. The catalogue of rivers is a memory technology, using the poem's formal properties — the alliteration, the meter, the sonic coherence of the list — to keep alive a geography that had no other record.

The Reveal and Its Meaning

After forty-three stanzas of cosmological disclosure, Odin begins to list his names.

Grímnir. Gangleri. Herjann. Hjálmberi. Þekkr. Þriðji. Þuðr. Uðr. Helblindi. Hárr. Saðr. Svipall. Sanngetall. The names accumulate — by the end of the tradition's full accounting, Odin has more than two hundred names, each encoding a specific aspect, function, or disguise. The list in the Grímnismál is shorter than the complete enumeration elsewhere, but its function here is specific: each name is a piece of evidence, and the evidence is directed at Geirröðr, who has been standing there listening and is now, stanza by stanza, beginning to understand what he has done.

He understands too late. Odin names himself directly — names himself Odin, the one who stands before the king — and Geirröðr, rising from his throne, stumbles on his own sword and falls on it. The poem disposes of his death in a single half-stanza. The death is not the point. It is simply what happens when a king whose reign depended on Odin's favor tortures Odin for eight days and then learns what he has done. The consequences are proportional and immediate and carry no dramatic weight, because from the moment the masked stranger was tied between the fires the outcome was never in question. The poem always knew how it ended. The only person who didn't was the king.

Agnarr — the young man who brought the water on the eighth day, the one act of human decency in the poem's frame — takes the throne. The Grímnismál's ethics are compressed into this transition: the one who recognized what was in front of him and responded to it appropriately inherits the kingdom. The one who didn't is dead on his own sword. The poem requires nothing more elaborate than this to make its point. Hospitality is not optional. Generosity is not optional. The stranger who comes to your hall might be the most powerful being in the nine worlds, and how you treat him is as consequential as it would be if you knew who he was.

The Grímnismál as Liturgical Resource

In contemporary Norse practice, the Grímnismál functions as a resource of a specific and practical kind: a source for the sacred names and places that populate ritual. The names of the divine dwellings are invoked in blót. The inhabitants of Yggdrasill appear in runic and seiðr work as cosmological reference points. The list of Odin's names — heiti, poetic epithets, each one a different face of the same god — provides practitioners with a vocabulary for addressing Odin in his various aspects, approaching the god through the specific name that corresponds to what is being asked or offered.

This liturgical function is not a modern invention imposed on ancient material. The Grímnismál was almost certainly used this way from the beginning — its lists designed not merely to transmit information but to enact it, to make the divine world present through the act of naming its parts. Saying the names of the rivers of Hvergelmir in a ritual context is not recitation but cartography — drawing the map of the cosmos in sound, in the presence of a community that needs to know where it is.

The Grímnismál is not the most dramatic poem in the Poetic Edda, nor the most emotionally complex. It does not have the prophetic grandeur of the Völuspá or the philosophical density of the Hávamál. What it has is completeness — a willingness to name everything that can be named, to leave no corner of the cosmos without a word attached to it. In a tradition where names have power, that is not a small achievement. The whole world, held in forty-four stanzas, spoken by a god in pain between two fires in a king's hall — and the world, when the king falls on his sword, still standing.

Chapter 9

Skírnismál: The Price of Desire

From the wrong seat, Freyr sees everything he should not.

He has climbed to Hliðskjálf — Odin's high seat, the throne from which the chief god surveys all nine worlds simultaneously — and from there he looks out over Jötunheimr, the realm of the giants, and sees Gerðr. She is walking from her father's hall to a smaller building, and when she raises her arms to open the door the light that comes off her skin illuminates the sky and the sea. Freyr watches her and something in him breaks.

The transgression embedded in this opening detail is worth pausing on. Hliðskjálf is Odin's seat, not Freyr's. Sitting there without permission is an act of presumption — the Norse equivalent of a junior officer occupying the general's chair. The tradition is clear on this: Hliðskjálf grants its occupant total cosmic vision, but that vision is calibrated for a mind that can handle omniscience without being destroyed by it. Odin can look out across all nine worlds and remain Odin. Freyr looks out and immediately loses himself. The seat shows him something true — Gerðr is real, her beauty is real, his response to her is real — but it shows it to him at a scale and intensity his nature cannot absorb. The desire that consumes him is not ordinary desire. It is desire amplified to a divine and fatal degree by the instrument through which he encountered it. He never had a chance.

He comes down from the seat and cannot speak. He cannot eat. He cannot sleep. He does not know yet that he will give away his sword for her — the sword that fights on its own when wielded by a man of courage, the sword without which he will be unarmed at Ragnarök when Surtr comes from the south and the fire begins. He does not know any of that yet. He only knows that he has seen something he cannot unsee, and that everything that follows is already decided.

The Skírnismál — "The Lay of Skírnir" — is the most psychologically uncomfortable poem in the mythological section of the corpus. Not because of its violence, though it contains some of the most concentrated curse poetry in the tradition. Because of its honesty about what desire does to the person who feels it, and what that person will do to obtain what they want.

The Structure: Three Movements

The poem divides cleanly into three movements, each with its own tone and function.

The first is brief and elegiac. Njörðr, Freyr's father, sends the servant Skírnir to find out what is wrong with his son. Freyr tells him: he saw a woman in Jötunheimr and he cannot have her, and he will not be well until he does. He asks Skírnir to go to her as his emissary — to cross into giant territory, to reach Gerðr, to bring her back. In exchange he offers Skírnir his horse — the one that rides through dark and through flame — and his magic sword. Skírnir accepts. The transaction is completed in a handful of stanzas, with the quiet finality of a decision that both parties know cannot be undone.

The second movement is the journey and the negotiation, and it is here that the poem's tonal range becomes fully apparent. Skírnir rides through the dark and the flame to Gerðr's father's compound, forces his way past the herdsman who challenges him, and enters. Gerðr receives him — not warmly, but without overt hostility. She asks what he wants. He tells her. She refuses. He offers gifts: eleven golden apples, the ring Draupnir that drips eight equal rings every ninth night, both of which she declines with a composure that is, in the circumstances, remarkable. Skírnir escalates. He threatens her with a sword — Freyr's sword, the sword that was the price of this mission. She does not yield. Then Skírnir carves runes — and what follows is unlike anything else in the corpus.

The Tamsvísur: The Darkest Magic

What Skírnir speaks over Gerðr is called in the poem tamsvísur — taming verses, verses of compulsion. They are the most sustained piece of operational curse magic in the Eddic tradition, and they read as if composed by someone who had thought very carefully about what it would take to break a person who did not want to be broken.

The curse works in layers. First Skírnir threatens Gerðr with death — with the sword that he still holds. She is unmoved, which tells him, and us, something about her: a specific kind of fearlessness that comes from valuing something — her will, her refusal, her autonomy — more than she values her life. Skírnir recognizes this and shifts his approach completely.

If death will not move her, he will make living intolerable.

The curse that follows is precise and escalating. She will be exiled to the world's edge, where she will sit on a mound at the entrance to Hel, watching the dead file past, unable to join them and unable to return. She will eat only goat dung and clay. No man will want her. Every being she encounters will turn away. She will be alone in a way that goes beyond physical isolation — cosmically, permanently, irreparably alone, visible to everything and connected to nothing. She will desire men but they will not come. She will have all the appetite of a living person and none of the possibility of satisfaction. She will be tormented by a three-headed giant whose name Skírnir carves into the wood while he speaks it, and the carving makes the words real in a way that speech alone cannot.

Then he carves a rune of madness — þurs, the rune associated with giants and with uncontrolled chaos — on her, and says he can uncarve it if she agrees. If she doesn't, he will add more. Gerðr agrees.

What the Curse Tells Us

The tamsvísur have generated significant scholarly discomfort, and that discomfort is legitimate. This is a poem in which a woman is threatened, when physical violence fails, with a magical curse designed to destroy her psychological and social existence until she submits to a marriage she does not want. The poem presents this as successful. It does not editorialize. It moves from the curse to Gerðr's capitulation to the arrangement of the meeting with the same flat narrative tone it uses for everything else, and then it ends.

Reading it honestly requires resisting the temptation to either normalize it or treat it as a simple moral lesson in how not to behave. The Skírnismál records what happens when divine desire encounters mortal resistance, with complete clarity and without endorsing the methods. Freyr's love for Gerðr is genuine — the poem never suggests otherwise — and its genuineness does not make what is done in its name acceptable. The transaction at its center is a coercion, and the poem does not look away from that fact.

The mythological frame complicates the picture without resolving the discomfort. Freyr is a Vanir god — a god of fertility, of the growing season, of the life-force that moves through the natural world. Gerðr is a giantess — a figure of the earth, of the cold ground that must be warmed and opened before it can receive seed. Their union is, at the cosmological level, a sacred marriage: the fertility god and the earth, the union without which the cycle of growth cannot begin. The Skírnismál encodes, in narrative form, the myth of the opening of the earth in spring — the ground that resists, that is cold and closed, that must be compelled before it yields. This interpretive frame contextualizes the poem's moral difficulty without resolving it — shows us that the violence in the narrative is a projection of the violence implicit in the agricultural cycle itself, the forced opening that is also a gift.

The third thing is to notice what Freyr pays, and what the payment means.

The Price

Among everything Freyr surrenders for Gerðr, the sword is what the tradition will not let him forget. In this tradition, a man's sword is his most personal possession — the weapon that carries his luck, that has been in battles he has been in, that is as much a part of his identity as his name. More than that: Freyr's sword is magical. It fights on its own. It is the instrument that would allow him to meet Surtr at

Ragnarök with any hope of matching the fire giant's power. Without it, he fights Surtr with no weapon of equivalent force, and falls.

The Skírnismál mentions this in passing, almost as a footnote — Skírnir names the sword as part of the price, Freyr agrees, and that is that. The Vafþrúðnismál confirms it from the other direction: at Ragnarök, Freyr fights and falls because he lacks his sword. The gap between the two poems is the space inside which the entire cost of desire lives. The gods generally know their fates — that is the tradition's assumption — so Freyr knows, at some level, that he is trading his survival for love. He makes the trade anyway.

This is the poem's deepest statement, and it is made without commentary. The poem does not moralize about Freyr's choice. It records the choice, records its consequence, and leaves the reader to sit with both. Whether Freyr's willingness to sacrifice his future for what he desires in the present is noble or foolish or both simultaneously is a question the Skírnismál declines to answer. It has done its job by showing the transaction clearly. What you make of it is your own business.

The choice is recognizable outside any mythological context. The thing you want badly enough to trade something you cannot replace — the future safety, the practical necessity, the thing that would have protected you if you'd kept it. People make these trades knowing the cost in advance, and that knowledge changes nothing about the choosing. Freyr sees Gerðr from Odin's seat and the arithmetic is already done. Everything after that is just the working out of a calculation that was complete in the first moment.

Gerðr's Silence

What Gerðr does not say after she agrees deserves as much attention as what she does.

The text gives her no interiority, no expression of how she receives the outcome she has been coerced into. She names the place where she will meet Freyr — Barri, the sacred grove — and she sets the date: nine nights from now. Then the poem closes. Skírnir returns to Freyr, tells him what was arranged, and Freyr responds with a lament about the length of time he must wait — nine nights being, apparently, an eternity when you are in the condition he is in.

Gerðr does not speak again. We do not know what she feels. We do not know whether what happens in Barri nine nights later is the beginning of something that resembles the sacred marriage of myth or a continuation of the coercion that produced the arrangement. The poem has used her as the object of the transaction — desired, resisting, overcome — and when the resistance is overcome it loses interest in her as a subject.

This deserves examination beyond the immediate text. The Skírnismál is not unique in the corpus in its treatment of female characters as figures whose interiority matters until the narrative no longer requires it — and then doesn't. What makes it stark here is the contrast between how fully Gerðr's resistance is rendered and how completely her capitulation erases her. She is present, coherent, composed throughout the poem's middle movement — declining gifts that most beings would not decline, facing threats that most beings would not withstand. She has been, in short, a person with a perspective that carries weight. And then the curse works, and the poem's attention moves immediately to Skírnir's return journey and Freyr's impatience. What the tamsvísur takes from her in the narrative is her refusal and the poem's regard for her simultaneously. Reading the Skírnismál honestly means sitting with that disappearance without explaining it away, and carrying the discomfort it produces into the rest of the corpus, where similar disappearances happen more quietly.

The Skírnismál as Magical Text

In the practical tradition of Norse magic, the Skírnismál has been read as a demonstration of magical technique — specifically, the technique of using runic curses to bind or compel. The tamsvísur are studied not merely as mythology but as a model for how verbal magic operates: the escalating structure, the specificity of the threatened harm, the carving of the rune that transforms spoken curse into physical inscription and thereby gives it a permanence that speech alone cannot achieve.

The þurs rune that Skírnir carves on Gerðr appears elsewhere in the tradition as a rune of compulsion and of the chaotic giant-force that disrupts order from below. Its deployment here as the instrument of psychological breakdown is consistent with its broader associations — it is a rune that works against the self, that turns the target's own mental and emotional architecture into the mechanism of their suffering. Skírnir does not overwhelm Gerðr from outside. He plants something inside her that will grow until she cannot bear it. The runic technology is psychological before it is magical, which is perhaps why it works when the sword does not.

This magical reading does not replace the mythological or psychological readings. It adds another layer to a poem that has always operated on multiple registers simultaneously — as fertility myth, as magical instruction, as psychological study, as moral provocation. The Skírnismál uses its apparent simplicity — short, clean stanzas, a clear narrative arc, a definitive ending — to contain something considerably more difficult than its surface suggests.

That difficulty is its value. The poems in the corpus that are easiest to summarize are rarely the most interesting to think about. The Skírnismál resists summary because its most important content is in what it doesn't say — in Gerðr's silence, in Freyr's wordless calculation, in the space between the curse and the capitulation where something that cannot be named in verse is happening to a person who deserved better.

The sword is gone. The meeting will happen. The grove is called Barri. Nine nights.

Chapter 10

Thor in Action: Hymiskviða and Þrymskviða

Comedy and theology are not opposites. In the Norse cosmos, they are the same instrument played in different registers.

Before we enter the two Thor poems that close the mythological section of the Codex Regius, that point needs making — because the temptation when reading the Þrymskviða, a poem in which the mightiest god in the Norse pantheon spends most of its length dressed as a bride, is to conclude that it is doing something lesser than the Völuspá or the Hávamál. It is doing something different, with complete craft and full awareness of what it is doing. The mythological corpus needs its comic poems the way a cathedral needs its gargoyles: not as decoration, and not as relief from seriousness, but as evidence that the tradition is large enough to contain everything — including the spectacle of a god in a veil eating an entire ox at his own wedding.

The Hymiskviða is the more straightforwardly heroic of the two, though it has its own ironic edges. Together they give us the fullest picture of Thor available in the Eddic corpus — a Thor considerably more interesting than either the earnest protector of the Völuspá or the buffoonish strongman of later comic tradition. He is powerful, sometimes ridiculous, occasionally embarrassed, and completely indispensable. That portrait is deliberate.

Hymiskviða: The Cauldron at the Edge of the World

The premise of the Hymiskviða is logistical. The gods want to hold a feast. Ægir, the sea giant who brews mead for the divine world, is pressed into hosting, but he lacks a vessel large enough to brew sufficient quantities for the entire pantheon. The solution: Thor and Týr will travel to the hall of the giant Hymir — Týr's father, which the poem mentions with the casual matter-of-factness the corpus uses for divine genealogies that would, if examined too closely, raise difficult questions — and retrieve from him a cauldron large enough for the purpose. The cauldron is described as a mile deep, which even allowing for mythological hyperbole suggests the gods plan to drink seriously.

What makes the Hymiskviða interesting is not its plot, which is simple, but its texture — the specific quality of attention it brings to the figures involved and the situations they navigate.

Hymir himself is one of the more fully realized giant figures in the corpus. He is enormous — his eyebrows alone, when he enters the hall and his glance crosses the beam where Thor is hiding, cause the beam to crack and the cauldrons hanging from it to fall. He is not stupid. He is not simply hostile. He is a father receiving an unwelcome guest, and his discomfort has the recognizable quality of a man who knows there is going to be trouble and is trying to manage it before it escalates. He feeds his guests. He takes Thor fishing. He sets tasks. He is doing, in the giant idiom, exactly what a host is supposed to do — testing a stranger, establishing hierarchy, offering what can be offered without surrendering what cannot. He is an antagonist in the technical sense: a force opposing the protagonists' goal, with his own perspective and his own reasonable concerns about having the God of Thunder in his hall eating his cattle.

The fishing sequence is the heart of the poem and one of the most striking set pieces in the corpus. Thor and Hymir go out in Hymir's boat. Thor rows them further than Hymir is comfortable going — out to the deep water, the outer ocean, the part of the sea that borders on Jötunheimr and beyond that on nothing. Hymir catches two whales and considers this adequate. Thor is not fishing for whales. He baits his hook with the head of one of Hymir's largest oxen — an ox he slaughtered before the trip, over Hymir's protests — and drops his line into the water below them.

What rises to the bait is Jörmungandr, the World Serpent, the creature that encircles Miðgarðr at the bottom of the ocean. Thor hauls it up. The serpent rises. Thor's feet go through the hull of the boat under the force of his effort and he stands on the ocean floor, bracing against the weight of something that contains the perimeter of the world. He raises Mjölnir. He is about to kill it.

Hymir cuts the line.

The serpent sinks back. Thor hurls Mjölnir after it — the poem is ambiguous about whether the throw connects — and Hymir sits in the boat, pale, having just done something that will cost him later but that he could not, in that moment, help doing. The giant who was managing the situation with reasonable competence could not manage this situation. The death of the World Serpent at the wrong time and in the wrong place would have consequences that even Hymir, no friend of the gods, apparently found too large to contemplate.

This encounter matters beyond this poem. The Völuspá establishes that Thor and Jörmungandr will kill each other at Ragnarök — Thor's appointed death, the serpent's appointed death, the mutual destruction that is their fate. The Hymiskviða gives us the dress rehearsal, the near-miss, the moment when the fated thing almost happens before its time and is prevented by a giant who doesn't fully know why he's preventing it, only that he must. Fate in the Norse cosmos is not simply what happens. It is what happens at the right moment. The serpent will die at Ragnarök because that is when it is meant to die. Hymir's cut line is the cosmos enforcing its own schedule.

The cauldron is obtained — Thor eventually, after additional trials, carries it home on his head, which is the poem's most purely comic image — and the feast can proceed. The Hymiskviða closes without ceremony, its business completed, its tone somewhere between heroic adventure and domestic comedy, a register it has occupied throughout with complete comfort.

Týr, it should be noted, loses both hands in the retrieval — one at the jaws of Fenrir, a detail established elsewhere, and the other, the poem implies, somewhere in the chaos of the exit from Hymir's hall. The poem mentions this almost as an afterthought. Týr is not the focus here, and his losses, considerable as they are, are noted and moved past. He is a god who has paid significant prices for the stability of the divine order and who receives, in return, relatively little narrative attention. The Hymiskviða is one of his larger appearances in the corpus, and even here he is supporting cast. His presence is essential to the mission; his experience of it is not the story.

Þrymskviða: The Most Comic Poem in the Corpus

The great god reaches for Mjölnir in the morning and it isn't there. The opening of the Þrymskviða is domestically immediate, and the poem never fully recovers its dignity from this beginning, which is the point. Something cosmologically fundamental has gone wrong, and the way it has gone wrong is inherently undignified: someone crept in while the God of Thunder was asleep and took his weapon. The theft is not presented as a military strike or a declaration of war. It happened quietly, in the night, and Thor woke up and it was gone.

The thief is Þrymr, king of the frost giants, who has buried Mjölnir eight leagues underground and will return it on exactly one condition: Freyja, the most beautiful of the goddesses, must be brought to him as his bride.

Loki is sent to negotiate. He borrows Freyja's falcon-shape and flies to Þrymr's hall, where the giant sits contentedly braiding his horses' golden manes and describes his happiness with the smugness of someone who believes he has already won. When Loki returns and reports the terms, Freyja's response is the most undisguised emotion in the mythological section of the corpus: she is so furious that the hall shakes and her famous necklace, the Brísingamen, flies off her neck. She will not be sent to Þrymr. The question of whether she is even being asked or simply informed is one the poem glosses over, but her reaction makes clear what she thinks of the proposition.

The gods hold council. Heimdallr — described here, in one of the poem's comic touches, as possessing foresight like the Vanir, which raises the question of which side of the divine family he actually comes from — proposes the solution. Thor will dress as the bride. Loki will dress as the bridesmaid. They will go to Þrymr's hall, retrieve the hammer when it is brought out for the wedding ritual, and then Thor can do what Thor does.

The poem gives Thor exactly one stanza of objection before he accepts. His concern is not safety or strategy — it is that the other gods will think him unmasculine. This is a very specific and very human anxiety for a deity of his stature to have, and the poem deploys it with evident pleasure. Loki's counter-argument is equally specific: without the hammer, the giants will overrun Ásgarðr. Against that, Thor's reputation can take the hit. Thor, who is not subtle but is not stupid, concedes the point.

What follows is the poem's sustained comic achievement, and it earns its comedy through precision rather than exaggeration. The bridal preparations — the veil, the keys at the belt, the women's dress falling to the floor — are described with the same detail the tradition uses for actual bridal preparations, which creates the comic effect through fidelity to the real thing rather than parody of it. Thor in a dress is funny because the dress is described seriously. The humor is in the gap between the form and its occupant, not in any distortion of the form itself.

At the wedding feast, Thor's behavior is a sustained diplomatic crisis. He eats an entire ox, eight salmon, and all the sweets set out for the women, and drinks three barrels of mead. Þrymr, watching this from across the table, wonders aloud about the bride's appetite. Loki, performing the bridesmaid's role with considerably more comfort than Thor is managing the bride's, explains that Freyja has been so excited about the wedding that she hasn't eaten in eight days. Þrymr accepts this. He leans over to kiss the bride and catches a glimpse of the eyes beneath the veil — eyes described as burning like fire — and pulls back. Loki explains that Freyja hasn't slept in eight days either, from eagerness. Þrymr, who appears to have entirely suspended his critical faculties, accepts this too.

The poem is not mocking Þrymr's gullibility. It is observing, with dry accuracy, what happens to a person who wants something badly enough: they stop checking the evidence. Þrymr has Freyja — or what he believes is Freyja — at his table. He wants this to be true so much that he looks past the ox, the salmon, the mead, the fire-eyes, the hands that are clearly a warrior's hands, the general impression of suppressed violence that a veiled Thor apparently radiates even at his most cooperative. Desire made Freyr give away his sword in the Skírnismál. Here it makes a giant not notice that his bride could break him in half.

Mjölnir is brought out for the wedding ritual — placed in the bride's lap, as was customary, to consecrate the union under Thor's own symbol. The central irony resolves in a single moment: Mjölnir, stolen to coerce the gods into surrendering their most prized goddess, is placed in the hands of the god it was stolen from. Thor grabs it. Þrymr and his entire hall die in the next four stanzas, briskly and without elaboration.

The Þrymskviða closes on Thor's sister, who expects a bridal gift and receives instead — the poem implies, without quite stating — a hammer to the head. The ending is abrupt and slightly startling, a reminder that the comic register and the violent one are not in different poems. They are in the same poem, occupying the same space, and the transition between them requires nothing more than a stanza break.

Two Poems, One God

Reading the Hymiskviða and Þrymskviða together produces a portrait of Thor that is more complete than either poem could deliver independently, and that portrait is worth sitting with before we move on.

Thor is not an intelligent god. The tradition does not ask him to be. He is powerful, loyal, reliable, occasionally impulsive, and capable of being manipulated — by giants, by Loki, by anyone who understands that his responses are predictable if you know what he values. What he values is simple: the safety of Miðgarðr, the protection of the divine order, the hammer in his hand and the problem in front of him. He does not strategize beyond the immediate situation. He does not accumulate wisdom at the cost of suffering, the way Odin does. He solves problems by hitting them, and when hitting them isn't the right tool, he is genuinely at a loss until someone — usually Loki — tells him what to do.

This is not a diminishment. Odin's way of being in the world is not presented as the only valid one, or even as the best one. Odin's wisdom costs him everything, constantly, and what he buys with it is always incomplete. Thor's simplicity costs him dignity occasionally and gains him something more durable: the uncomplicated trust of the people who live under Mjölnir's protection. The farmers who sacrificed to Thor were not asking for subtlety. They were asking for their crops not to be destroyed, their families not to be killed, their world to remain intact. Thor is the god that task requires.

The comic poems understand this. The comedy in the Þrymskviða is not at Thor's expense — it is in service of his function. A god willing to wear a dress and eat an ox in front of a hall full of giants to get his hammer back is a god who will do what is necessary, and who understands that the dignity is a small price against the cost of leaving without the hammer.

Mjölnir is returned. The wedding feast is a massacre, the order holds, and a god in a bridal veil who knew what he was doing has done it — which is neither a small thing nor a permanent one, only a thing that has been maintained, for now, at the price of a ruined dress and whatever the poem's final stanza implies about Thor's sister.

Chapter 11

Lokasenna: The Flyting of Loki

Everyone in the hall knows it has gone too far. The problem is that everything Loki is saying is true.

The Lokasenna — "Loki's Flyting," or more literally "Loki's Quarrel" — is the most explosive poem in the Poetic Edda, and its explosion is carefully engineered. Loki does not lose control at the gods' banquet. He arrives in control, stays in control, and leaves in control, having systematically dismantled the dignity of every god present with accusations that none of them can refute. The poem is sometimes read as a breakdown — the trickster finally burning every bridge, going too far, crossing a line he cannot uncross. Read it again. There is nothing uncontrolled about it. What looks like chaos is a precise operation, conducted by someone who has decided that the time for pretending is over and who knows which truths will land hardest and where.

What makes the Lokasenna extraordinary is not its violence — it contains almost no physical violence until the very end. It is the quality of the intelligence behind it, and what that intelligence reveals about a pantheon that the other poems present with rather more dignity than the evidence supports.

The Setup

The banquet belongs to Ægir, the sea giant, held in his hall beneath the waves. The gods are guests. The ale is excellent — the poem notes this with the specificity of someone who considers it relevant — and the gathering has the quality of a formal occasion going well: gods drinking together, receiving compliments from the serving staff, enjoying the particular warmth of a community at ease with itself. This is the divine order at its most self-congratulatory, and it is the specific mood Loki is about to destroy, because that mood is the problem.

He has been excluded from the feast. The precise reason is not stated, but the tradition elsewhere establishes that Loki's relationship with the divine community has been deteriorating for some time, and his exclusion here is consistent with a god who has been sliding toward the outside of the circle for reasons that the other poems in the corpus make clear. He arrives anyway, demands entry by invoking an oath Odin once swore that they would drink together or not at all, and is admitted. The oath is the key. Loki is not forcing his way in through strength — he is exploiting a promise that was made in a different context, when the relationship between him and Odin was different, when that kind of oath meant something different. He is using the old intimacy to gain access to the setting where he will destroy it.

He then kills a servant.

This is the detail that most readings of the Lokasenna move past too quickly, because the killing seems like a provocation rather than a statement. It is both. The servant Fimafengr has been receiving praise from the assembled gods for his skill and attentiveness, and Loki kills him for it. The act is irrational by any normal social calculus — you do not murder a servant at a divine banquet because the guests are complimenting him — and its irrationality is the point. Loki is announcing, before he says a word, that the normal social calculus does not apply tonight. He is here to break things. The killing is the opening move in a performance that will not stop until everything is broken.

He is driven out. He comes back. He asks for a seat and a drink. And then he begins.

The Flyting as Form

Before examining what Loki says to each god, the form deserves attention — because the flyting is more than an insult contest, and understanding what it is designed to do changes how you hear the accusations.

The flyting is a ritual verbal contest in which two parties exchange increasingly pointed challenges, boasts, and accusations. It appears across Germanic and Norse literature in various forms, from the Lokasenna itself to the exchanges between heroes before battle in the heroic poems. Its social function is complex: on the surface it is competitive entertainment, but it also serves as a truth-testing mechanism. The convention of the flyting is that the accusations made within it are expected to be grounded in reality — not mere invention, but the weaponization of things that are actually known or believed about the target. A flyting insult that is completely false lands with less force than one that is partially or wholly true, because the audience, which knows the tradition, can assess the accuracy in real time.

This is what makes Loki's flyting something other than simple destruction. In a conventional flyting, both parties attack with equal reciprocity and the winner is the one whose truths are more devastating. What Loki does is asymmetric: he does not defend himself against the gods' counter-accusations — in several cases he acknowledges them freely and immediately — because his goal is not to win the contest. He is not competing. He is testifying.

The Accusations: A God-by-God Reckoning

Óðinn is first and receives the most carefully calibrated blow. He is accused of practicing seiðr — the magic associated with women and with the feminine, whose practice by men was considered a form of ergi, a term covering unmanliness, cowardice, and sexual passivity simultaneously. For the chief god, the warrior-god, the god of masculine sovereign power, this accusation is devastating in a way that goes beyond the personal — it undermines the entire basis of Odin's authority, his identity as the supreme masculine principle in a value system that takes gender hierarchy extremely seriously.

Odin's counter-accusation — that Loki has also practiced seiðr, has lived as a woman, has borne children — is true, and Loki does not deny it. He simply points out that Odin is in no position to raise the subject. The symmetry is exact: both have done this thing; one of them is pretending he hasn't. The god of wisdom, of secret knowledge, of the long view — caught in the kind of hypocrisy that his own tradition should make him immune to.

Frigg is accused of having slept with Odin's brothers Vé and Víli while Odin was absent. The accusation locates itself in the Norse anxiety about a woman's conduct in the absence of her husband, and in the specific theological problem of what it means for the chief goddess to be implicated in a betrayal of the chief god. Frigg does not respond. Her silence is more eloquent than any counter-accusation she could offer.

Freyja is accused of having slept with every god and elf in the hall, and with her own brother Freyr. Freyja's sexual history is referenced elsewhere in the corpus without shame — she is a Vanir goddess for whom sexuality is a form of power, not a moral failing — but the Lokasenna's context transforms it into an accusation because the Æsir world has standards of feminine behavior that Freyja's conduct doesn't meet, and the poem is deploying those standards against her even as it refuses to endorse them. She knocks over a goblet and goes quiet. The woman who is never quiet — who wept gold tears for her lost husband, who is fierce and capable and fully present in everything she does — sits in silence at Ægir's feast and does not respond. This is as precise an image of the poem's effect as anything in the Lokasenna.

Skaði is reminded that Loki was involved in the killing of her father Þjazi — the event that defines her mythology, the wound that never fully heals. Þjazi's eyes, she is told, have been thrown up into the sky by Odin and made stars, which is meant to console her and which Loki implies she should be more grateful for, given the circumstances. She is not grateful. Her response is a threat — she will be permanently hostile to Loki — which he dismisses by reminding her that she was sweet enough toward him once, when she was trying to obtain Baldr's release from Hel. Whether the accusation is true is less important than what it does: it converts Skaði's grief into something that can be used against her, and it names the price she paid for a thing she failed to obtain.

Týr is told that his hand — the one Fenrir bit off when the gods tricked the wolf into accepting the binding — was lost in a transaction that did not serve him well, and that his wife has been sleeping with Loki. Týr cannot respond with force because he is missing the hand. He cannot respond with a counter-accusation that lands, because Loki is already moving on. The god of justice and of the law, whose sacrifice of his hand guaranteed the binding of Fenrir, is reduced in four lines to a cuckold who got the worst of every deal he made.

Bragi, the god of poetry and eloquence, receives perhaps the most pointed treatment: he is accused of cowardice. For the god whose domain is the celebration of heroic valor, this is not just an insult. It is an indictment of his entire function. The god of poetry who cannot be brave is a poet who cannot mean what he sings. Bragi threatens violence. Loki points out that threats from someone sitting down at a feast are unconvincing. Bragi, who is sitting down at the feast, cannot effectively respond to this.

Njörðr is mocked for the terms of his marriage to Skaði — the arrangement in which neither could tolerate the other's homeland, the sea versus the mountains, the compromise that satisfied no one. But the accusation goes further: Loki reminds him that he was once a hostage, sent to the Æsir by the Vanir in the exchange that ended the divine war. The god of the sea, of fishing, of the prosperous coast — revealed as someone who arrived in the divine community as a prisoner and who has been making the best of an uncomfortable situation ever since. Njörðr cannot deny this. Nobody in the hall can deny it. The hostage exchange is historical fact in the Norse cosmos. Loki is simply saying it aloud in a room full of people who agreed, by collective silence, never to say it.

Heimdallr is accused of having a wet and miserable existence as the eternal watcher on the gods' walls — always alert, always at his post, always watching for the threat that will eventually come regardless of how diligently he watches for it. The accusation is almost gentle by Loki's standards, which makes it more devastating: Heimdallr's entire function, his reason for existing, is reimagined as a form of chronic servitude. The sentinel reframed as the servant.

What Loki Is Actually Doing

The Lokasenna is sometimes read as Loki simply being destructive — the chaos principle finally running unchecked, burning what it touches because that is its nature. This reading is comfortable because it makes Loki's behavior explicable without requiring us to take his accusations seriously. If he is just being chaotic, the accusations are noise. If he is being precise, they are signal — and the signal is deafening.

Every accusation in the Lokasenna is drawn from the tradition — from stories that exist elsewhere, that the Norse audience would have known, that the gods themselves cannot deny because they are true. The flyting exposes not just the gods' individual histories but the contradictions in the value system they claim to embody. Odin preaches wisdom and practices deception. Freyja embodies desire and is shamed for it by a community that benefits from what she represents. Týr enforces law and was complicit in the deception of Fenrir. Bragi celebrates courage and cannot demonstrate it at his own table. The gap between what each god represents and what each god has actually done is where Loki plants his accusations, one by one, with surgical precision.

This is what makes the Lokasenna philosophically interesting rather than merely entertaining. Loki is attacking them not for being bad but for pretending to be better than they are — for maintaining the appearance of a divine order that their actual behavior consistently undermines. The banquet in Ægir's hall is a ceremony of divine solidarity and self-congratulation, and Loki is the one who will not participate in the ceremony. Not because he is outside the moral order — he is deeply implicated in it, has participated in it, has done favors for almost every god he now insults — but because he has stopped pretending that the ceremony means what it claims to mean.

The Lokasenna's Loki is not the Ragnarök Loki yet — not the architect of catastrophe, not the one who leads the giants' fleet against the gods. He is something more uncomfortable: the one who says what everyone knows but no one will say, in a setting where the saying of it cannot be undone. His outsider status, which has been building throughout his mythology, reaches its crystallization point here. He was always partly outside the divine community — born a giant, admitted to it, valued for his cleverness, used repeatedly for tasks the gods could not or would not do themselves. Tonight he is fully outside it, and he is using his outside position to say what can only be said from there.

The Arrival of Thor

Near the poem's close, Thor arrives and delivers an ultimatum: stop, or face Mjölnir. Loki does not stop immediately — he gets in one last observation about Thor's history with the giant Útgarða-Loki, a story of divine humiliation that Thor clearly does not want discussed — but then he leaves. His final words before departing acknowledge that he is leaving because of the hammer, not because Thor has won the argument. The distinction matters. The argument is unfinished. The force that stops it is physical, not logical. Loki has not been refuted. He has been silenced.

This is the Lokasenna's closing statement on the divine community. The gods cannot answer Loki's accusations. They can only produce someone large enough to make continuing the accusations inadvisable. Thor's hammer is the gods' real argument — the only one that works, and it works not by addressing anything Loki has said, but by making the consequences of continuing to say it too immediate to ignore. The poem records this without comment because the comment would be redundant.

The Binding of Loki

The frame narrative that surrounds the Lokasenna in the Codex Regius — probably a scribal addition rather than part of the original poem — describes what happens after Loki leaves the hall. He flees. The gods pursue him. He is eventually captured, bound in a cave with the entrails of his son Narfi, a serpent dripping venom on his face, his wife Sigyn holding a bowl to catch what she can. This is the binding we encountered in the Völuspá as one of the presages of Ragnarök — the event that locks Loki in place until the final battle, when he breaks free and leads the giants' fleet against Ásgarðr.

The Lokasenna is therefore not just a poem about a bad night at a divine banquet. It is the hinge point — the event that converts Loki from the gods' difficult but functional associate into their imprisoned enemy. What happens at Ægir's feast is the point of no return, for Loki and for the divine community. Before it, the relationship is strained but operative. After it, the machinery of Ragnarök begins to engage. The flyting is the moment the end begins.

Whether Loki caused this or whether the Lokasenna is the inevitable expression of a break that was always going to happen — whether he is the agent of the catastrophe or its symptom — is a question the tradition leaves open. The poem shows us what happened. The interpretation of why is the work it leaves for the reader.

Loki as Philosophical Figure

The Lokasenna raises a question it never answers directly: is the divine order that Loki dismantles worth defending?

As the poem makes clear, the gods are not the paragons of virtue that their official mythology presents. They are complicated, compromised, capable of cowardice and duplicity and hypocrisy, and Loki knows it because he has been with them from the beginning and has watched all of it. His accusations are not random — they are a systematic exposure of the gap between the gods' self-presentation and their actual conduct. The divine community of the Lokasenna is a community of beings who have agreed to maintain a certain fiction about themselves, and Loki is the one who refuses to maintain it.

The closest parallel in Western philosophy is the figure of Socrates in the Athenian agora — the man who walked into public spaces and asked the powerful to justify what they claimed to know, and who was eventually silenced not because he was wrong but because being right about powerful people's limitations has consequences. Loki at Ægir's feast is Socrates at a banquet he wasn't invited to, and the hemlock, when it comes, is administered in the form of snake venom dripped into a bound god's face. The parallel is not exact — Socrates did not murder anyone before making his philosophical points — but the structural position is the same: the truth-teller who makes himself intolerable to the community by refusing to pretend, and who is destroyed not by refutation but by force.

At the same time, the order he disrupts — however imperfect — is the order that holds Miðgarðr together, that keeps the giants from overrunning the human world, that maintains the conditions under which human life is possible. The chaos Loki represents is genuinely destructive. By the time the Lokasenna is finished and Loki is bound in his cave, the Norse universe is measurably closer to its end, and the people who will die in that ending are not only gods. They are the farmers whose crops Thor protects, the travelers who make offerings at crossroads, the ordinary inhabitants of a world that runs on divine maintenance and will stop running when that maintenance stops.

Loki is right about the gods. He is also, in every practical sense, catastrophically wrong about what his rightness costs. The two things are the same thing, seen from different angles, and the Lokasenna is the poem in which both angles are fully visible simultaneously.

That is a rare achievement in any literary tradition. Here it arrives as a drinking party that ends in chains and a prophecy of fire, spoken by a god who knew exactly what he was saying and said it anyway.

The gods at Ægir's table were not innocent. Nobody in that hall was. The Lokasenna knows it, Loki knows it, and by the poem's end, everyone listening knows it too. The question is what you do with that knowledge — whether you use it to burn the hall down, or whether you sit in the hall anyway, imperfect and implicated, and keep the serpent from the door.

The corpus contains both answers. It refuses to choose between them.

Chapter 12

Völundarkviða: The Smith and the Sky

He does not get his revenge by becoming a monster. He gets it by remaining exactly what he was before they broke him — which turns out to be far more terrifying.

The Völundarkviða is the last poem in the mythological section of the Codex Regius, and its placement there is quietly provocative. Völundr — known in the Anglo-Saxon tradition as Wayland the Smith, in German as Wieland — is not a god. He is described as álfa ljóði, prince of the elves, a semi-divine being of uncertain ontological status whose primary attribute is craft of surpassing skill. He does not appear elsewhere in the Eddic corpus in any significant way. He has no role in Ragnarök. He does not attend the gods' councils. He enters the collection for one poem, does what he does with complete and devastating efficiency, and flies away at the end into a silence the tradition never breaks. The poem offers no judgment on him. No divine authority steps in to condemn or vindicate what he has done. He disappears into the sky, and the sky closes behind him, and that is the end.

That ending — or rather, that non-ending — is the Völundarkviða's most deliberate statement, and understanding it requires understanding what kind of poem this is and what kind of figure Völundr represents.

The Three Brothers and the Valkyries

The poem opens in a register quite different from where it will end.

Three brothers — Völundr and his siblings Slagfiðr and Egill — live at the shore of a lake called Úlfsjár, hunting and skiing through the wilderness. They are princes of the elves, the poem says, rulers of something, though the nature of their domain is never specified. They find three valkyries sleeping on the shore, take their swan-cloaks, and the valkyries become their wives. This opening has the quality of a fairy tale — the magical women caught out of their element, the mortal or semi-mortal men who hold them, the years of happiness before the inevitable departure. For seven years the three couples live together. In the eighth year the valkyries begin to long for something. In the ninth year they are gone.

Loss is handled with the same compression the Eddic corpus uses for everything that cannot be adequately described. The brothers ski out in different directions looking for their wives. Slagfiðr and Egill do not return to the narrative. Völundr stays. He sits in his hall and waits and works — forging rings of red gold, seven hundred of them, strung on cords hanging from the rafters. Waiting for a return that the poem's frame tells us, without stating it, will not come. The rings are not practical objects. They are grief made physical, a craftsman doing what a craftsman does with what he cannot resolve through any other means. Into this hall of waiting, King Níðuðr comes.

Capture and Mutilation

Níðuðr comes for the gold and stays for the smith. The king and his men approach Völundr's hall while the elf-prince sleeps, count the rings, remove one — a detail that will matter later — and withdraw to consider their options. Níðuðr's daughter Böðvildr takes the ring for herself. Níðuðr takes Völundr's sword. When Völundr wakes and finds the ring missing, he assumes, with the specific readiness of a man who has been waiting for a particular person for nine years, that his valkyrie wife has returned. The hope in this assumption — the vulnerability it reveals in someone who has been forging grief into gold for years — is one of the poem's most precisely painful moments. He sits and waits. He falls asleep again. He wakes bound.

What Níðuðr does next situates the Völundarkviða in darker territory than almost anything else in the mythological corpus. He has Völundr hamstrung — the tendons at the back of his knees cut — and marooned on an island called Sævarstöð, where the smith is compelled to work exclusively for the king. The hamstringing is strategic, not incidental cruelty. Völundr cannot swim to shore. He cannot be rowed away without the king's knowledge. He is not imprisoned in a cell because a cell could theoretically be escaped. He is imprisoned in his own damaged body, in the middle of water, on a flat rock with a forge. The king has calculated that a lame man who cannot walk far is a man who cannot leave.

What the king has not calculated is what a man who cannot leave will do with enough time and sufficient motivation.

Níðuðr's wife, who appears only briefly but with a cold clarity that makes her presence felt throughout the poem, advises her husband to watch Völundr's eyes when the sword is mentioned — the sword taken from the hall. She has recognized something in the captive smith that her husband has not: that Völundr's stillness is not submission but waiting. The poem moves past her observation quickly, but it deserves attention. She is right. She sees what is coming before anyone else does, and her warning goes unheeded, and the thing she saw comes to pass. The Völundarkviða gives her no name and no further lines. It gives her the distinction of being the only character in the poem who understands what Völundr is.

The Revenge

The revenge is constructed in three stages. Together they constitute one of the most methodically planned acts of vengeance in the literature of any tradition.

Níðuðr's two sons come to the island to look at the treasures Völundr is crafting. He kills them. He makes goblets from their skulls — silver-mounted, sent to Níðuðr as gifts. He makes jewels from their eyes and sends them to Níðuðr's wife. He makes a brooch from their teeth and sends it to Böðvildr. The poem describes these acts with the same precise attention to craft that it uses for the ring-forging at the poem's opening. The sons' bodies become raw materials. The horror is not underlined. It is simply described, with the same neutrality the poem uses for the fishing and the waiting and everything else. This is the Norse technique of significant silence taken to its extreme: the more atrocious the act, the flatter the tone.

Böðvildr comes to the island with the ring — the one removed from the rafters, now broken. She wants the elf-prince to repair it, and she does not want her father to know. This visit, and what happens during it, is handled with a compression that is almost violent in its brevity. Völundr drugs her ale. He rapes her. She leaves the island pregnant. The poem allocates four lines to this. There is no commentary. The structure of the scene makes the nature of the act clear: she is unconscious, he acts, she wakes confused and weeping and does not fully understand what has happened to her.

This is the most morally unbearable section of the poem, and it is presented as part of the revenge without any signal that the tradition considers it differently from the killing of the sons. Böðvildr is not Níðuðr. She has done nothing to Völundr except bring a broken ring to someone she trusted to fix it. Her implication in the revenge is entirely a function of whose daughter she is, and the poem does not distinguish between her guilt and her father's.

What the Völundarkviða will not do, and what we should not do for it, is resolve this into a moral framework it does not offer. The poem records Völundr's actions without endorsing them — with the same flat exhaustive accuracy it brings to everything else — and leaves the reader to carry the weight of that recording. This is a specific choice, not aesthetic cowardice: to show the full cost of what was done to Völundr without softening what he does in return, and to trust the reader to hold both without being told what to think.

The Flight

Völundr has made himself wings. This detail is so matter-of-factly introduced — he forges wings the way he forges everything else, on the island, on the forge the king gave him to keep him productive — that it almost passes without registering. Of course he made wings. He is the greatest craftsman in the nine worlds. If a lame man needs to leave an island and cannot walk, a craftsman makes the thing that will take him off it.

He confronts Níðuðr from the air, hovering beyond reach, and tells him everything. The sons are dead. Their skulls are the cups on the king's table. The jewels the queen wears are their eyes. Böðvildr has been raped and is with child. Völundr names each thing with the patience of a man who has spent months or years planning this speech, wanting to be sure that Níðuðr understands the full accounting before he goes. Then, without waiting for a response, he flies away.

Níðuðr calls his daughter. She confirms what Völundr said — she was on the island, she drank ale, she does not fully understand what happened to her, only that it did and that she could not prevent it. The poem ends here. Not with Níðuðr's grief or his rage or any attempt at pursuit. With a young woman's confusion and her father's silence, and the sky where Völundr was.

The Archetype of the Smith

Völundr belongs to a figure that appears across multiple traditions and that consistently occupies the same uncomfortable position: the maker who is also the destroyer, the craftsman whose skill places him outside the ordinary moral categories by which other people are judged.

Daedalus builds the labyrinth that imprisons the Minotaur and the wings that kill his son. Hephaestus — lame, like Völundr, exiled from Olympus — forges the weapons of the gods and the net that catches Ares and Aphrodite in their adultery. Both figures are boundary-crossers: they make things that transcend the normal limits of what is possible, and they occupy a social position that reflects this — essential but marginal, valued for their output and uncomfortable in their presence. The smith knows things that other people don't, can do things that other people can't, and this knowledge makes him both indispensable and slightly threatening.

Völundr intensifies this archetype. He is not merely a craftsman displaced from his social position by lameness and exile. He is a craftsman who turns the materials of destruction — the bodies of children, the vulnerability of a young woman, the king's own greed — into instruments of a revenge so carefully crafted that it constitutes, in its way, his greatest work. The goblets made from the sons' skulls are technically accomplished objects, valuable enough to be sent as gifts, accepted and used before their nature is known. This is the smith's logic taken to its terminal extreme: anything can be made into something, if you know how.

The Moral of the Poem

The Völundarkviða does not offer one — not in the sense of a lesson or a judgment.

What it offers instead is a complete picture of what happens when a being of exceptional capability is subjected to exceptional injustice and given sufficient time and materials. The outcome is not heroic in the Norse sense — Völundr does not die well in battle, does not sacrifice himself for something larger, does not accept his fate with the dignity the tradition elsewhere prizes. He plans, he executes, he speaks, and he leaves. There is no drengskapr here in the conventional sense, no code of honor governing his conduct. There is only the cold arithmetic of harm received and harm returned, carried out with a craftsman's attention to detail and a craftsman's indifference to the emotional texture of the work.

The poem places this at the end of the mythological section not because Völundr belongs to the mythological world — he barely does — but because his story is the mythological section's final note, the one that undercuts the grandeur of what came before. After the cosmic sweep of the Völuspá, after the divine wisdom of the Hávamál, after Thor's heroics and Loki's devastating clarity, the collection closes with a lame man on an island, forging cups from children's skulls, and flying away without punishment and without redemption into a sky that tells us nothing.

The heroic poems that follow begin from a world that contains this possibility — and the weight of it never quite leaves the narrative.

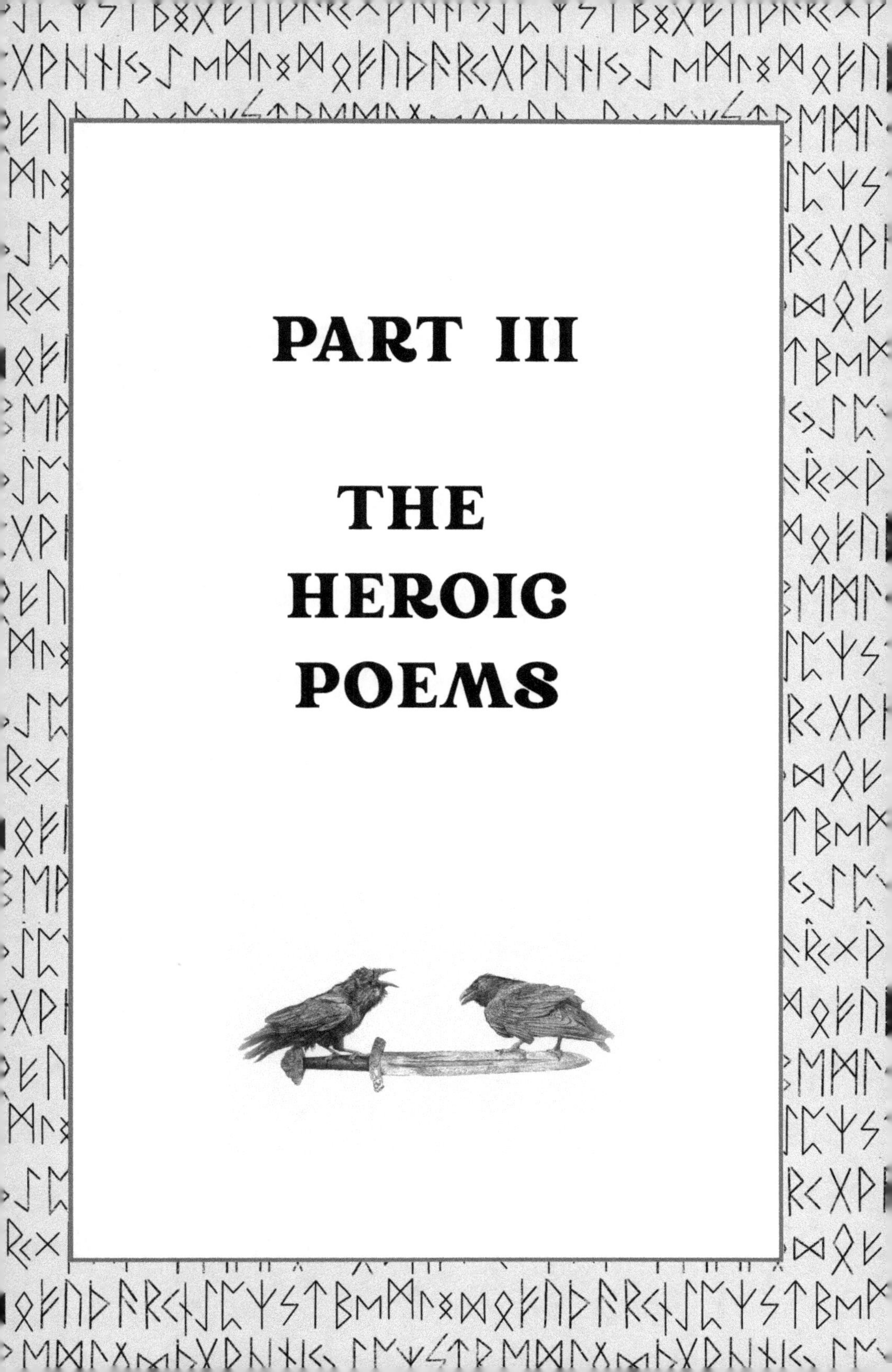

PART III

THE HEROIC POEMS

Chapter 13

The Hero Cycle: Why It Belongs Here

The heroic poems begin where the mythological poems leave them: in a world that is going to end.

This is not a metaphor. The Norse audience that listened to the stories of Sigurðr and Brynhildr, of Gunnarr and Högni, of Guðrún's terrible patience and Atli's greed, knew the cosmological frame within which those stories were set. They had heard the Völuspá. They knew about Ragnarök — the wolf, the serpent, the fire, the silence. They knew the gods were mortal. They knew the world was temporary. And into that frame, the heroic poems place human beings — or beings close enough to human that the distinction barely matters — and ask what it looks like to live a fully Norse life when you know the shape of things.

The answer is not pretty. But it is coherent, and its coherence is what this chapter is about.

The Question of Placement

Why do the heroic poems belong in the same collection as the mythological ones?

The surface answer is historical: the Codex Regius compiler put them together, and so they are together. But this is not an adequate answer for a compiler who was clearly making deliberate choices about what to include and in what order. The placement of the heroic cycle immediately after the mythological section — separated only by the great lacuna, the eight missing pages whose loss is permanent

— is not arbitrary. It is a statement about how the two bodies of material relate to each other.

The mythological poems give us the structure of the Norse universe: how it was made, how it is sustained, how it will end, what the gods are and what they are not. The heroic poems give us human beings — kings, warriors, valkyries, queens — moving through that structure without the gods' power or the gods' partial foreknowledge, navigating a world whose rules have been established by the first section of the collection. When Sigurðr walks into a dragon's lair, he is walking into a world where fate is as real and as operative as it is for Odin and Thor. When Guðrún watches her brothers ride into Atli's trap, she is watching the same force that will swallow Odin at Ragnarök — the force of what has been laid down, inexorable, before any of the players arrived.

The heroic poems are not illustrations of the mythological poems. They are the mythological poems' consequences, played out at human scale.

Örlög: The Woven Fate

The concept that ties the two halves of the Poetic Edda together is örlög — a word that resists clean translation but that the tradition treats as one of the most fundamental facts of existence.

Örlög is fate, but not fate in the sense of a plan someone made. The word's root is the combination of ór, meaning "from" or "out of," and lög, meaning "law" or "that which is laid down." Örlög is what has been laid down from the beginning — the pattern established before gods or humans existed, woven by the nornir at the base of Yggdrasill before the first morning of the world. It is closer to the structure of things than to any divine decree: the way cause produces consequence, the way the shape of a life produces the shape of its ending.

The nornir — Urð, Verðandi, Skuld, whose names approximate to "that which was," "that which is becoming," and "that which shall be" — carve the destinies of gods and humans into the wood of the World Tree. They do not create these destinies arbitrarily. They read what the structure of things requires and they name it. The distinction is subtle but crucial: örlög is inherent, not imposed from outside. The nornir are readers, not authors — beings who can perceive the pattern that was always already there and make it legible.

What this means for the heroic poems is that the tragedies they contain are not accidents. They are not the result of bad decisions that could have gone differently with slightly better information or slightly better choices. They are the working out of patterns established before the heroes were born. Sigurðr's death is not a surprise in this tradition. It is a destination — something the tradition knows is coming from the moment it tells us who Sigurðr is. The question the heroic poems ask is not whether it will happen. The question is who the heroes are while it happens, and that question is the one that matters.

The Norse Hero: A Different Species

The Norse hero differs from the hero of Greek epic not just culturally but structurally — the difference is built into the cosmological framework within which the heroic poems operate.

The Greek hero — Achilles, Odysseus, Heracles — exists in a world where divine intervention is genuinely possible. The gods take sides. They rescue their favorites from impossible situations. They grant extraordinary abilities, send favorable winds, whisper tactical advice in the hero's ear at critical moments. Even Achilles, whose death is fated, is given a choice about how and when — and his choice, famously, is to die young and famous rather than old and forgotten. The Greek tragic framework, at its most austere, removes divine intervention and allows fate to work. But the possibility of intervention is always lurking, which is why the absence of it, when it comes, is tragic in the specific Greek sense: the gods could have helped and chose not to.

Norse heroic poetry does not operate within this possibility. The gods do not routinely intervene to save human heroes. They may appear — Odin wanders through the heroic poems in various disguises, occasionally influencing events — but they do not rescue. The nornir have laid down the pattern. The pattern will be fulfilled. No god is going to cut the thread because a warrior prayed at the right moment or made the right sacrifice. This is not cruelty on the gods' part — it is the structure of a universe they themselves cannot override. Odin knows he will die at Ragnarök and cannot prevent it, so why should a human warrior expect better?

Christianity offers a different framework again. Redemption is possible. Suffering is not merely what happens to you — it is material that can be transformed, offered up, converted into something that transcends the immediate damage. The Christian martyrs die in the confidence that their deaths mean something beyond the deaths themselves, that what they are losing is temporary and what they are gaining is permanent. There is no equivalent mechanism in these poems. Death is death. What survives is reputation — the dómr, the judgment of the community — and reputation is a human artifact with no divine guarantee behind it.

This produces a specific kind of hero: one who acts with full integrity not because it will be rewarded, not because a god is watching and will intervene on behalf of the deserving, not because suffering will be transfigured into something better, but because that is what the hero is. The heroic ideal, in these poems, is about identity rather than outcome. You are what you do, and you do what you are, and the fact that doing it will get you killed changes nothing about the doing.

Wyrd and the Limits of Will

The Old English word wyrd — cognate with the Old Norse urð, the name of the first norn — is often translated as "fate," but it carries a more active sense than the English word suggests. Wyrd is not merely what happens to you. It is the force that shapes what happens, the current in the river of events that you can swim with or against but that you cannot escape and cannot redirect. The Norse heroic poems are full of characters who know their wyrd and act anyway — who are told, explicitly, that a specific course of action will end in their deaths, and who take that course of action without hesitation.

This is not stupidity, and the tradition does not present it as such. It is the expression of a specific value: that what you choose when you know the cost is the truest possible expression of who you are. The choice made under pressure, with full knowledge of the consequences, is the choice that reveals character. Sigurðr kills

Fáfnir knowing that the dragon's gold carries a curse. Gunnarr rides into Atli's hall knowing it is a trap. Hamðir and Sörli march against Jörmunrekkr knowing they will not come back. In each case the knowledge changes nothing. The hero does what the hero does.

What wyrd does not eliminate is responsibility. This is the crucial point, and it separates this understanding of fate from simple determinism. The fact that Sigurðr's death is fated does not mean that Guttormr, who kills him, is absolved of responsibility for the killing. The fact that the Völsung dynasty was always going to be destroyed by the gold's curse does not mean that Brynhildr's grief, Guðrún's loss, or Atli's greed are forces of nature rather than choices made by moral agents. Örlög establishes the frame. Within the frame, people choose. The choices are real. The consequences of the choices are real. The fact that the frame was established before anyone arrived to make choices in it does not retroactively transform the choices into fate.

This is a sophisticated position, and the heroic poems hold it without spelling it out. They show characters making choices within constraints they did not choose, in a world whose rules they did not make, and being fully accountable for those choices nonetheless. The tragedy of the heroic cycle is not that the characters had no choice. It is that they had choices, made them with their eyes open, and paid the full price.

The Two Cycles and What They Offer

Part III covers two distinct heroic cycles, and they are worth distinguishing before we enter them.

The Helgi poems — three poems dealing with the warrior Helgi Hundingsbane and his valkyrie Sigrún — are the more mythologically saturated of the two. Helgi's life and death are framed by his relationship with a valkyrie who chooses him, loses him, and waits for his return from the dead. The cycle's central concern is love — specifically, love across the boundary of death, love so strong that the tradition explicitly invokes the belief in reincarnation to explain how it continues. These poems are the most romantically focused in the corpus, and they give us the clearest picture of the valkyrie as an agent with her own perspective and her own emotional stakes, not merely a function of the divine machinery.

The Völsung cycle — six poems covering the story of Sigurðr, Brynhildr, Guðrún, and the destruction of the Gjukungs — is the larger and more complex of the two, and the greatest sustained tragic work the corpus contains. A family tragedy on a cosmic scale, in which the curse on Andvari's gold contaminates everything it touches, pulling everyone who comes near it toward destruction regardless of individual virtue or vice. The Völsung cycle contains some of the most psychologically complex characters in medieval literature anywhere in Europe, and its central figures — Brynhildr above all — deserve to be read with the same seriousness we bring to the great tragic heroines of the Greek tradition.

Together, the two cycles cover the full range of what this heroic tradition understood heroism to involve: the warrior who fights and loves and dies, the woman who endures and acts and survives or doesn't, the community that destroys itself through the interaction of individual integrity and collective catastrophe. Something harder to name than cautionary tales or romances — a sustained meditation on what it costs to be fully what you are in a world that was never designed to accommodate you comfortably.

The mythological poems told us what the world is. The heroic poems tell us what it is like to live in it — and that is a distinction this corpus takes more seriously than almost any other body of literature from its time.

Chapter 14

The Helgi Poems: Love Beyond Death

The Codex Regius contains a note that has no parallel anywhere else in the manuscript. It appears between the two poems about Helgi Hundingsbane, inserted by the scribe in his own voice, and it says this: it was believed in ancient times that people could be reborn, though this is now called old wives' tales.

The qualification at the end — "though this is now called old wives' tales" — is a thirteenth-century Christian scribe doing what Christian scribes did: creating distance between himself and the pagan material he is preserving. But the note itself is remarkable. The scribe felt compelled to explain something about these poems that the poems themselves don't explain, which means he understood that the belief in reincarnation was not incidental to the Helgi cycle but central to it. Strip it out, and the story of Helgi and Sigrún becomes simply a tragedy — a warrior dies, a woman grieves, that's the end. Leave it in, and the story becomes something stranger and more durable: a love that refuses the boundary that everything else in this tradition treats as absolute. Death, in these poems, is an interruption, not a conclusion.

The Three Poems

The Helgi cycle comprises three poems, though the third — the Helgakviða Hjörvarðssonar — is a separate tradition that the compiler attached to the other two because of thematic overlap rather than narrative continuity. Its Helgi is a different figure from Helgi Hundingsbane, and its valkyrie — Sváva — is a different figure from Sigrún, though the structural pattern is the same: a valkyrie who chooses a warrior, names him, loves him, loses him. The repetition is deliberate. The compiler is pointing at something the tradition understood as a type — a recurring pattern in the relationship between the human and the divine worlds, specifically in the relationship between mortal heroes and the women who move between those worlds.

The two Helgakviða Hundingsbana poems are the primary texts. They cover the life of Helgi from birth through his battles, his love for Sigrún, his death, and what comes after his death. Together they run to several hundred stanzas, making the Helgi cycle one of the longer narrative sequences in the corpus, and they give more sustained attention to character interiority than almost anything else in the Eddic collection — more space given to dialogue, more willingness to slow down and let a moment accumulate weight before moving on. The compiler who valued compression above almost all else made room for these poems to breathe, which suggests he understood what they were doing differently from the poems around them.

A Prodigious Birth

The Norns come to the hall where Helgi is born and spin his fate by torchlight — the traditional image of the nornir at work, the spinning and weaving that fixes a life's pattern before the life has properly begun. They give him his name. They give him Hundingsbane as his destiny — the killer of Hundingi, the king who will become his defining enemy. They stretch the threads of his fate across the sky and fix them under the moon, which is the poem's image for a fate that is cosmic in scope, far beyond the personal. The life being outlined here will not be lived quietly or obscurely.

The prodigious birth is a standard feature of the heroic tradition — Sigurðr, Gunnarr, Hamðir all arrive with their destinies partially pre-established — but the Helgi poem gives it unusual weight. The nornir's work at the birth is not formulaic scene-setting. It establishes the central tension of the entire cycle: Helgi's life is fated, his ending is fated, and yet his relationship with Sigrún — which the tradition will insist on calling love, real love, the kind that persists across death — is also somehow fated, somehow part of the pattern the nornir are spinning. The two things are in tension with each other. A fated death and a love that defeats death cannot both be true simultaneously. The Helgi poems hold the tension without resolving it, which is what makes them interesting.

Helgi grows up fast, as Norse heroes do — the tradition does not linger on childhood, which is liminal and uninteresting to a culture focused on the moment of full social emergence. He fights his first battle young, kills Hundingi, begins the process of building the reputation that the nornir outlined at his birth. He is fearless, skilled, politically intelligent — a complete hero in the Norse sense, the kind of young man around whom other men gather because his proximity feels like luck.

The Valkyrie's Choice

Sigrún finds him first. This is the detail the Helgi cycle returns to repeatedly and that distinguishes it from most other love stories in the corpus: Sigrún is not found by Helgi. She sees him from wherever valkyries go when they are not on the battlefield, and she chooses him. The choosing is the act. She rides to him. She names herself. She tells him she has been given in marriage by her father to a man she does not want, and she asks Helgi to prevent the marriage by force.

This is the valkyrie's power in its clearest expression. She is a figure of the boundary between life and death, between the divine world and the human one, and her most characteristic act is this: choosing. Choosing which warriors die in battle and which survive, choosing which of the dead are taken to Valhöll, and here, choosing which living man she will love. The choice is sovereign. It is not qualified by her father's wishes or by the social conventions of the human world. She sees Helgi, she decides, and everything that follows from that decision is the poem's subject.

The marriage she is trying to escape is to Höðbroddr, a king whose family becomes Helgi's primary enemy through the poem's middle section. The battles that follow — and there are several, described with the Eddic tradition's characteristic mix of heroic inventory and compressed violence — are nominally political, the standard stuff of Norse heroic narrative: alliances, betrayals, flyting before combat, the enumeration of the dead. But in the poem's deeper logic they are the working out of

Sigrún's choice. By choosing Helgi, she has set in motion a chain of consequences that will define the rest of his life and the manner of his death.

She is not unaware of this. The valkyrie who chooses a mortal is choosing someone who will die — possibly because of her choice, certainly despite it. The tradition does not present Sigrún as naive about what she is doing. She is doing it anyway. This is the heroic logic applied to a female figure: she knows the cost and she pays it, which is exactly what the male heroes do in every other poem in the corpus. The Helgi cycle extends that logic across the gender boundary and does not make a fuss about having done so.

The Hamingja: Luck as Substance

The Helgi cycle introduces a concept that runs through the heroic poems more broadly but is most explicitly articulated here: the hamingja. The word is usually translated as "luck" or "fortune," but this translation flattens something more specific. In the Norse understanding, hamingja is not good fortune in the statistical sense — the run of favorable events that benefits some people and not others. It is a substance, a force that resides in a person and can be transmitted from one person to another, transferred at death to a successor or a descendant, sensed and assessed by those who know how to look for it.

Helgi has hamingja in abundance. This is what Sigrún perceives when she first sees him — not just his physical presence or his reputation, but the quality of his luck, the sense that events will arrange themselves around him in favorable configurations, that he is a person in whom the force of fortune is concentrated. Hamingja is not moral virtue. It is not reward for right conduct. It is something more like grace in the pre-theological sense: an unearned gift that some people have and others don't, that makes everything they touch go better than it should.

When Helgi dies — killed by Dagr, Sigrún's brother, in an act of revenge that the poem frames as obligatory from Dagr's perspective and devastating from everyone else's — the question of where his hamingja goes is not abstract. The scribe's note about reincarnation is directly relevant here: if Helgi is reborn, his hamingja is reborn with him, and the pattern of luck and love and destined death begins again.

The tradition is suggesting something specific about the nature of what Helgi and Sigrún are to each other: they are not two individuals who happen to love each other. They are a pattern, recurring, finding each other across the membrane of death and rebirth because the pattern requires it.

The Return from the Tumulus

After Helgi's death, one of his servants sees a company of horsemen riding toward the burial mound. He recognizes Helgi among them. He goes to Sigrún and tells her. She goes to the mound and enters it, and inside she finds Helgi — alive enough to speak, to touch, to share a cup with her. Alive enough for the poem to describe their reunion with the warmth of something not qualified or distanced by the fact that he is dead. He is there. She is there. For one night, whatever death has made of him, it has made of him something that can come back.

The scene is the most intimate in the mythological and heroic corpus. Eddic poetry prefers the significant silence, the compressed gesture, the meaning implied rather than stated. The Helgi poem breaks this pattern, and the break feels earned. This reunion — the living woman and the dead warrior in the burial mound, the darkness outside, the horses waiting — has a quality unlike anything else in the collection. It is quiet in a tradition of violence, tender in a tradition of compression, specific where everything else is general.

The scene also does something unusual with the Norse conception of the afterlife. In most of the corpus, the dead are simply gone — to Hel, to Valhöll, to whatever realm their manner of death assigned them — and the living do not follow them there and they do not return. The Völuspá describes Baldr's death and the silence after it without any suggestion that the living can reach him or that he can reach them. The Helgi poem insists otherwise. The burial mound is permeable. A dead warrior can ride back to it, and the woman he loved can enter it and find him there, and for one night the boundary holds itself open. This is a specific belief — the scribe's note confirms it was recognized as such — about the persistence of love across death, and the poems treat it not as folk superstition but as cosmological fact.

She asks him if she can ride with him. He says he must be gone before dawn, when the cock crows in Valhöll. She waits for him to return. He does not. The servant watches for him on subsequent nights, and finds nothing. The second Helgakviða Hundingsbana closes without resolution — no reunion in the afterlife, no promise of future meeting, no consolation. There is the burial mound and the darkness and the cock that crowed before he could come back a second time.

She grieves. The poem is brief about it, which is right — grief at this magnitude resists description and the poem does not try. What it gives us instead is the fact of her waiting, and then the silence after the waiting, and then the end.

Sigrún and the Valkyrie Tradition

The Helgi cycle gives us the fullest portrait of a valkyrie as an emotional being — as someone with desires and losses and a perspective on her own situation — available in the Eddic corpus. Valkyries elsewhere are primarily functional: they ride the battlefield, they select the dead, they appear occasionally in the mythological poems as divine instruments rather than independent agents. Sigrún occupies a different position in the tradition.

Her choosing of Helgi is an act of will that the poem respects as such. Her grief at his death is not presented as inappropriate or as a deviation from the valkyrie's proper function. It is simply her response to something she has lost, and the poem gives it space. The corpus, which treats grief primarily as something to be contained and redirected into action — as Guðrún's grief will be redirected in the Völsung cycle — allows Sigrún her grief without turning it into anything else. She is not told to act on it. She is not told to channel it. She grieves, and the poem ends.

This matters beyond the Helgi cycle. It establishes a template for how the heroic poems will handle female experience: not as secondary or instrumental to the male hero's story, but as its own thing, with its own weight and its own claim on the reader's attention. Sigrún does not exist to motivate Helgi's battles or to illustrate his virtue. She exists in her own right, and the poem knows it.

The Helgakviða Hjörvarðssonar: The Pattern Repeats

The third poem in the cycle — technically a separate story, but placed here deliberately — confirms that what we have been watching is not a singular event but a recurring structure.

Helgi Hjörvarðsson is born into obscurity: his father's favorite son, but nameless, incapable of speech, until Sváva the valkyrie appears on a mountain ridge and names him. The naming is the activation — without it, Helgi is incomplete, a hero in potential only. Sváva gives him his name and with it his identity, his capacity for action, his place in the world. She then disappears, and he spends the rest of his life trying to deserve the name she gave him.

He earns it, becomes a warrior of the necessary caliber, and finds Sváva again. They love each other across whatever distance separates the human world from the valkyrie's domain. He dies in a duel he could have avoided — honor required him to fight, so he fought — and as he is dying he sends word to Sváva, telling her to love another man. She refuses. The poem ends with both of them holding to what they are, past the point where holding to it does either of them any good.

The compiler who placed this poem beside the Helgi Hundingsbane cycle understood what he was doing. Two Helgis, two valkyries, two loves that cross the boundary between worlds, two deaths that the love survives and cannot survive simultaneously. The pattern repeating is the point. This is the tradition saying: this is how it goes, this is how it always goes, this is the shape of this particular kind of love in this particular kind of world.

The nornir spun Helgi's fate under the moon at his birth. They included Sigrún in that spinning, though the poem does not say so directly — her presence in his life, her choice of him, the reunion in the burial mound, are all part of the pattern. Fate, in this tradition, is not merely the outline of events. It is the texture of a life: who finds you, who loses you, who waits for you in the darkness after, and for how long.

Whether the repetition consoles or devastates is a question each reader answers alone.

Chapter 15

The Völsung Cycle I: Dragon, Gold, and Curse

Pull a thread from the Nibelungenlied, the Middle High German epic composed around 1200, and you arrive at the same place as pulling a thread from Wagner's Ring cycle, composed six centuries later. Pull either of those threads long enough, and you arrive here — at a cluster of Old Norse poems preserved in the Codex Regius that are older than both, stranger than both, and considerably less interested in making the story palatable than either. The Norse Völsung cycle did not soften its material for a courtly German audience, as the Nibelungenlied did. It did not reshape it into a four-opera meditation on power and love and the death of the gods, as Wagner did. It told the story the way the story went, in the tradition that first gave it shape, and what it preserved in doing so is the version closest to whatever original the tradition was working from.

Sigurðr kills a dragon, bathes in its blood, understands the language of birds, is warned by those birds of a betrayal, and rides on toward his fate anyway. That sentence is the Völsung cycle's first movement, and it contains multitudes.

The Protagonist and His Sword

Sigurðr is the greatest hero in the Norse corpus. This is not a casual claim — the tradition makes it explicitly, in multiple poems, through the mouths of multiple characters, and it means something specific. He is not merely the most powerful fighter, though he is that. He is the most fully realized expression of what the tradition means by a hero: the combination of physical force, clarity of purpose, generosity, and the willingness to act in the face of full knowledge of what acting will cost him.

His origin story is compressed into a handful of stanzas in the Grípisspá — a poem structured as a prophecy delivered to Sigurðr by his uncle Grípir, who tells him his entire life in advance. This is a remarkable device: the hero of the cycle is given a complete preview of his own story, including his death, before any of it happens. He listens. He objects, briefly, to the part about Brynhildr and the forgetting-potion and the betrayal. Grípir tells him the prophecy is fixed. Sigurðr accepts this, thanks his uncle for the truth, and rides away toward the events he has just been told will destroy him. The Grípisspá is sometimes dismissed as a late and artificial addition to the cycle — it is probably later than the other poems — but its function is essential: it establishes from the beginning that Sigurðr's tragedy is not a matter of ignorance. He knows. He goes anyway. That combination is the whole of what this tradition means by heroism.

His sword is Gramr — "Wrath" — the reforged sword of his father Sigmundr, which Odin shattered when Sigmundr's time was done. The reforging is performed by Reginn, the dwarf-smith who becomes Sigurðr's foster-father and who has his own reasons for wanting the sword restored. A sword that Odin broke is a sword that belonged to Odin's dispensation: not merely a weapon but a symbol of divine favor granted, withdrawn, and granted again in a new generation. When Sigurðr tests the reforged Gramr on Reginn's anvil and cuts it in two with a single blow, the scene is one of those moments in the corpus where poetic compression operates at maximum intensity — a detail that would require pages to explain in prose, conveyed in two stanzas, complete.

Fáfnir: The Dragon Who Speaks

Before Fáfnir was a dragon, he was a dwarf — Reginn's brother — who transformed himself into one to guard the gold he had stolen from their father Hreiðmarr. Hreiðmarr had received that gold as blood-payment from the gods for the death of his son Ótr. The gold itself was stolen from the river-dweller Andvari, who cursed it as it was taken. The curse moves with the gold, from Andvari to Hreiðmarr to Fáfnir to everyone who will touch it after. This is the Völsung cycle's engine: not malice, not accident, but a curse embedded in an object, passing from owner to owner, doing what curses do.

Fáfnir chose his transformation. He became what he needed to be to keep what he wanted to keep. The dragon is not a monster who stumbled into his role — he is a being who traded everything else he was for the certainty of possessing this one thing. When Sigurðr digs a pit in the path Fáfnir takes to the water and waits for the dragon to pass over him, he is not meeting a force of nature. He is meeting a choice — the extreme terminus of a specific kind of desire, the thing that desire becomes when it has consumed everything else.

The dialogue between Sigurðr and the dying Fáfnir is one of the most striking exchanges in the corpus, and it deserves more attention than it usually receives. Fáfnir does not rage at his killer. He does not beg for mercy. He warns Sigurðr. He tells the young hero that the gold will be his death, that everyone who touches it will be destroyed, that the curse is real and operative and cannot be outrun. He speaks with the authority of someone who has known the gold's nature from the inside and who no longer has any reason to conceal it. Sigurðr's response is that a man must die some day, and that dying rich is better than dying poor. This exchange is the cycle's central philosophical position in miniature: the knowledge of destruction does not constitute a reason to refuse the thing that will destroy you, because the thing is real and the future remains theoretical until it arrives.

The dragon-slaying is also a study in the mechanics of inherited conflict. Reginn is not a disinterested party. He is Fáfnir's brother, and his father Hreiðmarr was killed by Fáfnir for the gold. He has raised Sigurðr as a foster-son with exactly this outcome in mind: a hero strong enough to kill the dragon, controllable enough to be used. The birds that warn Sigurðr of Reginn's betrayal are not revealing something unexpected. They are confirming what the structure of the situation already implied — that a man who uses another man as a weapon eventually has to dispose of the weapon, because a weapon that knows it has been used is dangerous.

Sigurðr processes this information and acts on it with the same decisive simplicity he brings to everything. Reginn is dead before the gold is loaded on the horse.

What the episode reveals is the difference between Sigurðr's clarity and the muddy motivations of everyone around him. He is not naive about Reginn's intentions — the birds make sure of that — but he is also not cautious in the way a calculating person would be cautious. He kills the betrayer and moves on, not because he has made a careful assessment of the threat, but because betrayal in this tradition has a specific and immediate consequence, and Sigurðr is a man who lives by the tradition's rules without apparent internal conflict. This directness, which makes him the most heroic figure in the cycle, is also what makes him vulnerable to the more complex machinations that await him among the Gjukungs. He is not equipped for the specific kind of harm that is coming — not because he lacks intelligence but because his intelligence operates in a register that the harm does not.

Sigurðr roasts Fáfnir's heart to test if it is cooked — Reginn has asked him to prepare it — and burns his finger on the juices. He puts his finger in his mouth. The dragon's blood gives him the ability to understand the language of birds, and the birds above the heath are saying several things simultaneously: that Reginn plans to betray him, that the gold is cursed, that Brynhildr the valkyrie sleeps behind a wall of fire on the mountain of Hindarfjall, and that Sigurðr should take the gold and ride to her. The sword goes with him. The gold goes with him. The curse goes with him.

The Sigrdrífumál: Knowledge on the Mountain

What Sigurðr finds behind the wall of fire is not quite what the later tradition makes of it.

The figure who sleeps in armor on Hindarfjall is identified in the prose frame of the poem as Brynhildr — and in the later tradition, in Snorri's prose and in the Völsunga saga, she is definitively Brynhildr. The poem itself calls her Sigrdrífa, a name that means something like "victory-driver," and leaves the identification somewhat ambiguous. Whether Sigrdrífa and Brynhildr are the same person is one of the standing scholarly debates of the cycle, and the ambiguity may be original rather than accidental — a deliberate elision connecting two narrative strands that were not originally the same story.

She is a valkyrie who was put to sleep by Odin as punishment for defying his will in battle — she gave victory to the wrong king, the one Odin had decided should lose, and Odin responded by declaring that she would sleep until a man fearless enough to cross the fire woke her. Sigurðr has crossed the fire. She is awake. And before anything else — before they speak of love or future or the complications that will follow — she teaches him the runes.

The Sigrdrífumál is the second great runic text in the Poetic Edda, after the Hávamál's Rúnatal, and it approaches the subject from a different angle. Where Odin's acquisition of the runes is about the cost of knowledge — the self-sacrifice, the nine nights, the falling back screaming into the world — Sigrdrífa's teaching is about application: what the runes do, where they are carved, how they are used. Victory runes on the sword hilt and the blade. Birth runes on the hands of the midwife and on the joints of the mother's arms. Wave runes on the prow and the steering oar. Healing runes on the bark of trees, on the east-facing wood, on the ground. Thought runes and speech runes and mind runes for the one who wants to be wiser than other men.

The catalogue is specific in ways that suggest genuine practical knowledge, or at least a genuine tradition of practical application the poem is drawing from. These are not the runes as cosmic structure, as in the Rúnatal, but operational runes — tools for specific purposes in specific situations. The teaching Sigrdrífa gives Sigurðr is a complete runic education delivered in the space of a morning on a mountain, which is either the poem being economical with narrative time or the tradition's understanding that the right teacher, in the right moment, can transmit everything that matters in a single session.

She ends the runic catalogue with general wisdom — advice on conduct, on restraint in speech, on the management of relationships with allies and enemies — that echoes the Hávamál's gnomic section in its concerns if not in its voice. The voice here is a valkyrie's, which gives it a different quality: wisdom delivered from a position of partial divinity, by a being who has seen battles from both sides of the threshold between life and death, to a man who will need everything she can give him for what is coming.

The poem breaks off. The prose frame tells us that Sigurðr and Sigrdrífa pledged themselves to each other on the mountain. What comes next — the forgetting-potion, the false marriage, the tragedy — is in the poems that follow.

Andvari's Gold: The Curse as Structure

The gold that Sigurðr takes from Fáfnir's lair has a history that precedes the Völsung cycle and that explains why the cycle's destruction is so thorough and so unavoidable.

The Eddic poem Reginsmál — the Lay of Reginn, which precedes Fáfnismál in the cycle — tells the backstory. Andvari was a dwarf who lived in a waterfall in the shape of a pike, and who had accumulated a vast hoard of gold including a specific ring, Andvaranaut, which had the property of generating more gold. Loki caught him and forced him to give up the gold as ransom for the life of Ótr — the otter-son of Hreiðmarr whom Loki had killed accidentally, not knowing it was a transformed human. Andvari gave everything, including the ring, and as it was taken from him he cursed it: the gold would be the death of every man who owned it.

Andvari is not a god with the authority to implement divine justice — he is a dwarf with a grievance, and his curse is an act of impotent rage that turns out to have real power. This is characteristic of the Norse understanding of cursing: the words spoken at the moment of loss, in genuine extremity, carry force because the extremity itself charges them. The curse does not require a deity's backing. It requires a specific quality of feeling at a specific moment, and Andvari had both.

What the curse does to the gold is not quite what a modern reader might expect. It does not corrupt it or make it visibly dangerous. It simply ensures that everyone who possesses it will be destroyed by it. The mechanism varies: Hreiðmarr is killed by his sons for it. Fáfnir becomes a dragon to guard it and is killed by Sigurðr for it. Sigurðr will be killed for it by the people he shares it with. The Gjukungs will be killed for it by Atli. The curse moves through the gold's owners like a pattern that each new possessor thinks will not apply to them, because the previous owners' destruction was caused by their specific flaws and circumstances. The next owner's destruction will be caused by theirs.

This is the cycle's understanding of what we might now call structural evil — harm embedded in an object or a system, operating independently of the intentions of the people who engage with it. Sigurðr is not greedy in the way Fáfnir was. The Gjukungs are not murderous by nature. None of them need to be particularly bad people for the curse to work. They need only to be in contact with the gold, and the gold will find the specific lever in each of them that produces the destruction the curse requires.

The Norse Cycle and Its Descendants

The Völsung cycle traveled far from Iceland. In the German-speaking world it arrived as the Nibelungenlied — a courtly epic composed around 1200 that takes the same basic story and relocates it in a world of medieval chivalry, softening the mythological frame and redistributing the moral weight. Brynhildr, the Norse tradition's most complex and most tragic figure, becomes Brunhild — still formidable, but reduced in philosophical significance. Sigurðr becomes Siegfried, still heroic, but embedded in a courtly romance that changes what his heroism is for. The curse of Andvari's gold becomes the treasure of the Nibelungs, still operative, still lethal, but stripped of its explicitly cursed quality — it is wealth that causes greed rather than a supernaturally contaminated object that causes destruction regardless of the moral quality of its possessors.

The difference matters. In the Eddic version, good people are destroyed by the gold because it is cursed. In the German version, people are destroyed by the gold because they are greedy, envious, or politically ambitious. The Eddic version is more theologically rigorous in its way: it does not require moral failure to produce catastrophe. The catastrophe is structural. The Nibelungenlied moralizes the story in ways the Norse poems deliberately refuse. What Wagner took from both traditions — the ring as central symbol, the curse, the fire, the tragedy — he put in service of a philosophical framework that is neither Norse nor German but distinctively his own, reflecting his specific nineteenth-century preoccupations more than anything in the original material.

Reading the Eddic poems after Wagner, or after the Nibelungenlied, requires deliberately setting aside what those later versions did with the material. They are great works on their own terms. As guides to what the Norse poems were doing, and why, they are unreliable.

The Moment Before the Fall

The Sigrdrífumál ends on a mountain, with a pledge and a runic education and the kind of morning the corpus rarely permits its heroes — uncomplicated, full of light, the future still theoretical. Everything Sigurðr needs is in place: the sword, the gold, the knowledge, the love. Grípir has told him what comes next. The birds told him before that.

He rides down from the mountain toward the Gjukungs, toward the forgetting-potion, toward Brynhildr and Guðrún and the catastrophe that will be completed in the next cluster of poems. The gold rides with him. The curse is patient. It has waited this long.

There is a specific quality to this pause — the moment between the hero's formation and his destruction — that the tradition understands and that the Sigrdrífumál holds with unusual delicacy. The teaching on the mountain is complete. The pledge is made. Nothing has gone wrong yet. The runes are carved. The sword is sharp. The dawn is breaking over Hindarfjall and Sigurðr is everything the tradition has built him to be, and for this one morning, before the gold reaches where it is going, that is enough.

It will not be enough for long. It was never going to be.

Chapter 16

The Völsung Cycle II: Brynhildr and the Fall

There is a moment in the Sigurðarkviða in skamma — the Short Lay of Sigurðr — when Brynhildr laughs.

She is in her bower, and she has just heard Guðrún weeping over something, and she goes to find out what it is. Guðrún tells her: Sigurðr is dead. And Brynhildr laughs. The poem records the laugh and moves on without explaining it, which is the correct decision, because the laugh is not explainable in any register that would reduce its complexity. It is not cruelty — Brynhildr loved Sigurðr and the poem does not let us forget this for a moment, even in the middle of the revenge she engineered. It is not relief — she will be dead within the poem's next section, by her own choice. It is something that has no adequate name in English: the sound made by a person who has arrived at the furthest possible extreme of a situation they themselves created, who knows exactly what they have done and what it cost, and who cannot find any other response equal to the full weight of the knowledge.

That laugh is the center of the second half of the Völsung cycle, the pivot on which everything before it turns and from which everything after it falls.

The Forgetting-Potion and Its Aftermath

When Sigurðr rides down from Hindarfjall into the world of the Gjukungs, he carries with him a pledge to Sigrdrífa — or Brynhildr, if they are the same — and the full runic wisdom she gave him, and the gold with its curse. What he does not carry, and cannot carry, is immunity from what happens next.

The Gjukungs — the royal family into whose orbit he falls — include Gunnarr, Högni, and their sister Guðrún. Their mother is Grímhildr, a woman of extraordinary magical skill and a clear-eyed pragmatism that the cycle treats without moral comment and without evident warmth. She sees Sigurðr and she sees the political and social advantage of binding him to her family. She prepares a drink that contains, among its other properties, a drug of forgetting. Sigurðr drinks it. He forgets Sigrdrífa. He forgets the pledge on the mountain. He looks at Guðrún and loves her, with the specific completeness of a man who has no competing memory.

The forgetting-potion is the cycle's most morally complicated device, and it is worth slowing down on. Sigurðr does not choose to forget. He is not choosing Guðrún over Brynhildr — the choice is made for him, without his knowledge, by a woman who understood that his free choice would not produce the outcome she wanted. The tragedy that follows is therefore built on a foundation of manipulation: every subsequent decision Sigurðr makes is made in ignorance of his own history, every subsequent relationship he forms is formed by a man who is, in a literal sense, not himself.

The cycle does not treat Sigurðr as a victim, nor Grímhildr as a villain in any simple sense. It treats the forgetting-potion as a cause, traces its effects through the system, and shows what the effects produce. The moral framework is causal rather than judgmental: this happened, therefore that happened, therefore this — and the audience is left to perform the moral assessment without explicit guidance from the poem.

The forgetting-potion also raises a question about memory and identity that the structure of the cycle implies rather than asks directly: if a man forgets who he is and what he has pledged, is he still the same man? The Sigurðr who marries Guðrún is Sigurðr in body and in the capacities that make him extraordinary — the strength, the skill, the clarity of purpose, the willingness to act. But he is not Sigurðr in history. He is a version of Sigurðr with a piece of himself missing, operating in the world without access to the specific memory that would most change his choices. The tragedy of the Völsung cycle is not simply that good people are destroyed by a curse. It is that the most fully realized hero in the tradition is reduced, at the critical moment, to a partial version of himself — and that partial version is sufficient to bring everyone around him to ruin, including himself.

The Lie at the Ford

What follows is the nuptial arrangement that completes the disaster. Gunnarr wants Brynhildr. She is surrounded by a wall of fire that only the most exceptional of men can cross — a detail that, if she is Sigrdrífa, means the fire is the same fire Sigurðr already crossed. Gunnarr cannot cross it. Gunnarr's horse will not cross it. Sigurðr's horse Grani could cross it, but Grani will not carry Gunnarr.

Grímhildr resolves this with a second piece of magic: she gives Sigurðr the shape of Gunnarr. Sigurðr-as-Gunnarr crosses the fire, reaches Brynhildr, and spends three nights beside her with a sword laid between them. He takes from her the ring Andvaranaut — the ring of the gold, the ring of the curse — and carries it back. Brynhildr agrees to marry Gunnarr. The exchange is complete. The cycle has placed the curse where it needs to be: in the hands of a woman who does not yet know what was done to her, married to a man who could not have obtained her without a deception she will eventually discover.

What Brynhildr does not yet know is vast. She does not know that the man who crossed the fire was not Gunnarr, that the man capable of crossing it is now her husband's brother-in-law, that she pledged herself on Hindarfjall to the man now married to someone else. She is living inside a deception so complete that she cannot even identify what is wrong, only that something is.

The Quarrel at the River

The deception breaks open at a ford, in one of those small domestic moments the heroic poems use to ignite catastrophe. Brynhildr and Guðrún wade into the river to wash their hair, and the question of whose husband is preeminent produces the argument that produces everything else. Brynhildr says Gunnarr is the greatest of men. Guðrún says Sigurðr is greater. Brynhildr says Gunnarr crossed the fire to win her — no man but he could have done it. Guðrún says it was not Gunnarr but Sigurðr in Gunnarr's shape, and she shows Brynhildr the ring Andvaranaut as proof.

There it is. In the water, between two women washing their hair, the complete structure of the deception laid out with no ambiguity and no possibility of retreat. Brynhildr knows now what was done to her. She knows that the man she was pledged to, the man who crossed the fire, is alive and married to the woman standing in front of her. She knows that her own marriage was obtained through a lie. She knows that the sword laid between them for three nights was a gesture of fidelity to a pledge that was subsequently wiped from Sigurðr's memory by a drug.

She goes pale. She goes home. She goes silent. And then she begins to plan.

Brynhildr: The Tragedy's Center

Brynhildr is the most complex figure in the Völsung cycle, and among the most complex in medieval literature of any tradition. She is neither villain nor victim, though the cycle gives her the structural position of both at different moments. She is something harder to categorize: a person of extraordinary capability and integrity, trapped in a situation that her own choices and other people's deceptions have produced, who responds to the trap by doing the most destructive thing available to her and who understands, completely, what she is doing.

She engineers Sigurðr's death. She goes to Gunnarr and tells him that Sigurðr has broken his oath of brotherhood — that he boasted of having spent the three nights with her not as Gunnarr but as himself. This is a lie. The sword was between them. But it is a lie that Gunnarr, who has his own reasons for finding Sigurðr's removal convenient, is not unwilling to believe. He persuades his brother Guttormr — who swore no oath to Sigurðr and is therefore free to act — to kill the sleeping hero. Sigurðr dies in his bed, or in the forest, depending on which version of the cycle you follow. Guðrún wakes beside his body.

Multiple poems in the cycle do not give a single consistent account of Brynhildr's motivation, and this inconsistency is itself meaningful — it reflects a tradition grappling with a character too complex for any single explanation to contain. In the Sigurðarkviða in skamma she is cold and strategic, moving through her revenge with the precision of someone who has thought it through completely. In the Brot af Sigurðarkviðu — the Fragment of a Sigurðr Lay, partially recoverable from what the lacuna left behind — she is more openly passionate, the grief and the anger closer to the surface. In the Helreið Brynhildar she is retrospective and almost judicial, recounting the facts of her own life with the dispassion of someone making a final report. She is the same person in all three versions and a different person in all three versions — the closest the corpus comes to acknowledging that a character of this complexity cannot be held in a single poem.

Why does Brynhildr do this? The cycle gives multiple answers, none of them reducible to the others. She does it for honor — Sigurðr, as she understands it, took her honor by crossing the fire and by taking the ring, regardless of whether the sword was between them. She does it for love — the poem makes clear, in the extraordinary Helreið Brynhildar, that she has loved Sigurðr from the beginning and that her grief at his death is as real as her role in causing it. She does it because there is no other option available to her in a world where what was done to her cannot be undone and where the only form of justice she has access to is the form she administers herself.

The Sigurðarkviða in skamma gives her a speech before Sigurðr's funeral that is one of the most sustained pieces of self-accounting in the corpus. She describes, in unapologetic terms, what she is, what was done to her, what she has done in response, and what she plans to do next. She plans to die on Sigurðr's funeral pyre. She will be burned with him, with the sword between them, as it was in the three nights on Hindarfjall. The speech is not repentance. It is completion.

The speech is delivered while Guðrún is sitting next to Sigurðr's body, weeping. Brynhildr's relationship to that grief — to the woman who told the truth at the ford and thereby set in motion the chain of events that killed the man they both loved — is not resolved in the poem. It is present, charged, unresolvable. Two women who have been used by the same system, whose conflict was manufactured by that system, sitting on either side of the body of the man the system destroyed. The cycle does not suggest they could have been allies. It places them there and lets the silence do its work.

The Helreið Brynhildar: Last Words

The Helreið Brynhildar — "Brynhildr's Ride to Hel" — is the shortest poem in the Völsung cycle and among the most concentrated pieces of verse in the corpus. Brynhildr, dead, is riding her wagon toward Hel. She passes a giantess who challenges her: what right does she have to this road, what has she done to deserve the death that brings her here?

Brynhildr answers. In a compressed sequence of stanzas she tells her own story from the beginning — the battle she fought, the defiance of Odin's will, the sleep on Hindarfjall, the fire, the deception, the murder she commissioned, and the choice to die. She is not claiming innocence. She is establishing the record — making sure that someone, even a hostile giantess on the road to Hel, understands what actually happened rather than the version that served the people who used her.

The Helreið is also, in its way, an answer to the Lokasenna — the poem in which Loki strips away the gods' pretensions and leaves them with no adequate defense. Brynhildr on the road to Hel is doing something similar for herself: refusing the version of her story that would reduce her to a jealous woman who destroyed a hero out of wounded pride. She is insisting on the full account, the one that includes what was done to her before she did anything to anyone. The corpus is not generally sympathetic to self-pity, and the Helreið is not self-pity — it is something more like testimony, delivered to an audience that did not ask for it, in a context where it cannot serve any practical purpose, simply because the record should be accurate.

Her final gift from the tradition that used her as the pivot of its greatest tragedy is this: the space to tell it from where she stood, without mediation or interruption. What she tells is not flattering to anyone, including herself. But it is true, as she knows the truth, and the poem treats the telling of it as itself a form of completion. She arrives at Hel. Sigurðr is already there, and whatever comes after is not the poem's concern — it has done what it came to do.

Guðrún's Lament

The first Guðrúnarkviða contains one of the most quietly devastating images in the entire corpus. Guðrún is sitting beside Sigurðr's body, unable to weep — the grief is too large for tears, or the shock has closed the channel. The other women in the hall try to help her: they tell her their own stories of loss, their own dead husbands and brothers and sons, each offering their grief as a kind of gift, an invitation to share the language of mourning. None of it works. Then one woman — Gullrönd, Gjuki's daughter — pulls back the shroud from Sigurðr's face and places Guðrún's hand on his cheek. Guðrún looks at him and weeps. The image of the hand on the dead face, the permission finally given to the body to acknowledge what has happened — this is the Guðrúnarkviða's great moment, shown rather than explained, trusted to carry its full weight without annotation.

Guðrún does not die with Sigurðr. In a tradition where the ideal response to a husband's death might be the pyre, Guðrún survives, and her survival is the condition for everything that follows in the cycle. The three Guðrúnarkviður are not uniform in tone: the first is immediate and devastated; the second is retrospective, Guðrún in exile at the court of a foreign king, telling her story from the beginning; the third is later still — Guðrún contemplating further loss, the survival that keeps producing new material for mourning.

What the Guðrúnarkviður establish is the figure who will dominate the final movement of the cycle: a woman who has lost everything she loved, who has not died, and who will eventually stop grieving and start acting. The grief is real and the poems give it full weight. But the Völsung cycle is not finished with Guðrún, and the curse on the gold is not finished with any of them.

The Atlakviða and the Atlamál — the poems that close the heroic section — will show us what Guðrún becomes when the grief has run its course. What she becomes is something the corpus regards with a specific kind of awe: a woman who has moved through total loss and arrived on the other side of it as something that cannot be contained by the ordinary categories of heroism or villainy. We are not there yet. For now, there is the body, and the fire, and the woman who laughed, and the woman who wept, and the sword laid between two people who should have been together and were not, and the gold still moving through the world with its curse intact, patient as ever, looking for its next hand.

Chapter 17

Atlakviða and Atlamál: The Last Songs

Reading the Atlakviða and the Atlamál in grœnlenzku back to back produces something close to double vision: the same events, the same characters, the same catastrophic arc, rendered in aesthetic languages so distinct from each other that the contrast becomes its own kind of commentary. The same story, told twice, in ways that reveal how much of a story lives in the telling rather than the events.

The Atlakviða — the Lay of Atli — is considered by many scholars to be among the oldest poems in the corpus. Its language is archaic, its syntax compressed to the point of obscurity in places, its imagery dense and allusive, its emotional register almost entirely suppressed. It moves through the destruction of the Gjukungs and the revenge of Guðrún with the speed and economy of something that has been told many times before and trusts the audience to bring the rest. It does not explain. It does not pause. It does not mourn. It narrates.

The Atlamál — the Greenlandic Lay of Atli — is probably later, possibly composed in Greenland (the title suggests it, though scholars debate this), and it reads like a different tradition's engagement with the same material. It is expansive where the Atlakviða is compressed. It is domestic where the other is epic. It gives characters interior lives — thoughts, hesitations, conversations overheard — that the Atlakviða does not. It mourns. It lingers. It is, in ways that would have been surprising to the tradition that produced the Atlakviða, novelistic.

Together they are the corpus's most explicit demonstration of something it shows everywhere implicitly: that there is no single correct way to tell a myth. The story is the story. How you tell it is a choice, and the choice reveals as much as the story does.

The Historical Core

Behind both poems is a historical event, or at least a historical tradition.

Attila the Hun died in 453 CE, reportedly of a nosebleed on his wedding night to a Germanic woman named Ildico. The circumstances were suspicious enough that contemporaries suspected foul play — that Ildico killed him. Whether this is what actually happened is lost to history. What matters for the Eddic tradition is that the story of a Germanic woman who destroyed the man she was forced to marry embedded itself in the collective memory of the Germanic peoples and traveled with them through the migrations of the fifth and sixth centuries, accumulating mythological weight as it went.

By the time it reaches the Eddic corpus, the historical Attila has become Atli, a figure with enough overlap with the original to be recognizable but enough difference to be fully legendary. The process by which historical events become mythological material here is not gradual distortion — it is active transformation, the tradition taking a piece of history and asking what it would mean if the people involved were the kinds of people it values, operating according to its rules. Atli is not a geopolitical actor in the poems. He is a specific kind of antagonist: the man who destroys what he cannot possess, who mistakes the gold for the point when the gold was never the point.

The historical Ildico has become Guðrún, the widow of Sigurðr, carrying the full weight of the Völsung cycle's grief and the full force of its curse. The historical nosebleed — if it was a nosebleed — has become a banquet of children's flesh and a burning hall and a woman walking into the fire. This tradition never domesticated its sources. It intensified them.

Atlakviða: The Epic Version

A messenger opens the poem, carrying Atli's invitation to the Gjukungs — to Gunnarr and Högni, Guðrún's brothers — couched in the kind of generosity that is recognizable, to anyone who has read the corpus this far, as a trap. Guðrún sends a warning: a runic message, or in some versions a ring wound with wolf's hair. The warning is decoded too late, or not decoded correctly, or decoded correctly and dismissed. The brothers ride to Atli's hall knowing, at some level, what is waiting for them.

This is the heroic logic the previous chapter established, applied now to figures who are not the central hero of the cycle but who embody the same principle. Gunnarr and Högni know this is probably a trap. They go anyway, because not going would be a failure of a different kind — a surrender of identity, a choice to be smaller than what they are. The poems do not present their decision as foolish. They present it as the only decision available to men of their specific quality.

At Atli's court, the trap is sprung. The Gjukungs fight with the ferocity that the tradition requires — the Atlakviða's battle sequence is one of the most concentrated pieces of heroic combat in the corpus, names and deaths accumulating with a speed that mirrors the actual experience of large-scale violence — but they are outnumbered and eventually captured.

Atli wants the gold. Specifically, he wants Andvari's gold, which Sigurðr brought from Fáfnir's lair and which the Gjukungs now possess. The invitation to his court is not primarily personal vengeance — it is a retrieval operation, and the Gjukungs are obstacles between him and the object he wants.

Gunnarr will not tell him where the gold is hidden while Högni lives — he says he has sworn to reveal it to no one while his brother breathes. Atli cuts out Högni's heart and brings it to Gunnarr as proof. Högni laughed while his heart was being cut out — the Atlakviða notes this with the same flat tone it uses for everything, and the detail is one of the corpus's most concentrated images of the heroic ideal: a man who greets his own death with laughter, not because he is unafraid but because fear is not the appropriate response to dying as yourself. Now Gunnarr is the only one who knows where the gold is. He tells Atli that it will stay hidden. He will take the knowledge to the grave, and he does — thrown into the snake-pit, playing his harp with his feet because his hands are bound, playing until the snakes take him.

Gunnarr in the snake-pit has become one of the defining images of the Norse heroic tradition, and it carries that weight for good reason. It appears not only in the Atlakviða but in the Atlamál, in later saga literature, in visual art — carved on runestones, depicted in the carved portals of Norwegian stave churches centuries after the conversion to Christianity. A man playing a harp with his feet in a pit of snakes is an image that lodges itself and does not leave, which means the tradition recognized in it something it needed to keep. What it keeps is the ultimate expression of the heroic principle: that identity is not something you maintain only when circumstances permit. Gunnarr in the snake-pit is exactly who Gunnarr was at the feast and on the road and in the battle and in the negotiation with Atli. The pit changes nothing about him. He plays because playing is what he does, and he does it until the snakes take him.

Guðrún's Revenge

Gunnarr's death in the snake-pit is the mistake the Atlakviða treats as both inevitable and fatal for Atli — because it is the moment Guðrún stops waiting.

Guðrún has been patient through Sigurðr's death, through the grief of the Guðrúnarkviður, through the forced marriage to Atli, through years of living in the hall of the man responsible for her brothers' deaths. The patience is not forgiveness. It is preparation — the stillness of someone who is waiting for the right moment with complete certainty that the moment will come.

What Guðrún does is total. She kills her own sons by Atli — the children she has had with the man she is about to destroy — and serves them to him at a feast. She tells him what he has eaten. She kills him. She burns the hall. The poem does not spare any of this. It narrates each act with the same flat economy it has used throughout — children, feast, murder, fire — and then it ends.

What the Atlakviða asks of its reader at this point is considerable. Guðrún killing her sons is not presented as the act of a woman driven mad by grief — it is a deliberate choice made by someone in full possession of herself, and the poem treats it with the same flat narrative respect it has given to every other act of violence in the text. The tradition is not comfortable with this, exactly — no tradition is comfortable with the killing of children — but it is not flinching from it either. It is insisting that the logic of total revenge, once entered into, has no stopping point short of total destruction. Guðrún does not stop at Atli. She does not stop at the hall. The poem stops only when there is nothing left to destroy.

The Atlakviða's restraint here is its final and most devastating technique. By refusing to respond emotionally to what it has just described — by offering the burning hall and then silence — it places the full weight of response on the reader. There is no authorial voice to tell you whether Guðrún is monstrous or heroic or both. There is only what happened, stated in the fewest possible words, and then the silence in which you are left to sit with it.

Atlamál: The Domestic Version

The Atlamál tells the same story and tells it differently in almost every particular.

Where the Atlakviða gives us Guðrún as an almost mythological figure — the instrument of a revenge so complete that it approaches the impersonal — the Atlamál gives us Guðrún as a person, living in a hall, dreading what she cannot prevent, warning her brothers in explicit terms rather than runic ones, grieving in real time rather than in the compressed retrospect of the older poem. She is human in the Atlamál in ways the Atlakviða does not allow her to be, and the humanity makes the revenge more disturbing rather than less — because we have seen what she felt before it, and we understand that the woman who kills her sons is not a figure of myth but a woman who loved those sons and who made a specific and deliberate choice about what mattered more.

The Atlamál also gives Högni a wife — Kostbera — and Gunnarr a wife — Glaumvör — who both read the warning correctly and try to prevent the fatal journey. Kostbera decodes Guðrún's runic message and tells Högni what it actually says. He dismisses her. Glaumvör has prophetic dreams and tells Gunnarr what they mean. He dismisses her. Both women, unnamed in the Atlakviða because that poem has no room for them, receive full scenes in the Atlamál, and their presence changes the moral texture of the story considerably. The brothers are not simply walking into a trap with heroic indifference. They are ignoring the warnings of people who love them and who are right. The Atlamál is interested in this failure of listening in a way the older poem is not.

The battle at Atli's court is longer in the Atlamál, more detailed, more attentive to the specific experiences of specific people. Guðrún herself fights alongside her brothers — she arms herself and enters the fray, a detail absent from the Atlakviða — and the fighting is described with the kind of attention to physical circumstance that the older poem never provides. The revenge, when it comes, is the same in its outlines, but rendered with a psychological precision the Atlakviða deliberately avoids. In the Atlamál, Atli speaks after he learns what he has eaten. He argues with Guðrún. He makes claims about what she has destroyed. She responds. The exchange between them is the Atlamál's most novelistic passage — two people having, in the most literal possible sense, their final conversation, each making the only argument they have left.

Oddrúnargrátr: The Story Behind the Story

The Atlamál and Atlakviða are the cycle's main event, but a third poem — the Oddrúnargrátr, the Lament of Oddrún — casts a different light on the same material by approaching it from an angle the other two poems never consider.

Oddrún is Atli's sister. She loved Gunnarr — the man her brother will destroy — and their love was prevented by Atli, who considered Gunnarr an unsuitable match or simply too useful as a political object to be given away in marriage. The poem is structured as a lament delivered by Oddrún to a woman she is helping through a difficult childbirth, and it consists largely of her account of her own story — how she loved Gunnarr, how the love was blocked, how they found each other anyway in secret, how Atli discovered it, how it ended.

What the Oddrúnargrátr does to the Atlakviða and Atlamál is give Atli a fuller context. The man who sends the fatal invitation to the Gjukungs, who orchestrates the deaths of Gunnarr and Högni, who provokes Guðrún's total revenge — he is also a man who prevented his own sister from marrying the man she loved, for reasons the poem doesn't fully specify but that feel political and cold. Atli the destroyer of families was also, first, a destroyer of his own family's happiness. The curse of the gold reaches him too, eventually. But he was already a particular kind of man before the gold arrived.

The Oddrúnargrátr is rarely discussed alongside the Atlakviða and Atlamál because its tonal register is so different — quieter, more intimate, more focused on private grief than on epic destruction. But the compiler placed it in the sequence deliberately. It is the Völsung cycle's reminder that the catastrophe has more than two sides, and that the people who are not at the center of the story have stories too, complete and painful and their own.

Two Aesthetics, One Story

The coexistence of these two poems in the Codex Regius rewards thinking about what the compiler was doing by placing them together.

Why was the Atlamál composed at all — what need it served, what the tradition felt was missing from the older poem — is worth sitting with. One answer is geographical and temporal: a poem composed in Greenland, for an audience distant from the original context of the Atlakviða, needed to supply more of the framework the older poem could assume. An Icelandic or Norwegian audience steeped in the tradition could follow the Atlakviða's compressed references; a Greenlandic audience may have needed the fuller account. Another answer is aesthetic: the Atlamál was composed because someone felt that the Atlakviða's restraint left something out — that the human texture of the disaster deserved more space. Both answers can be true simultaneously.

The compiler was not choosing between them. He was not presenting one as the correct version and the other as a variant. He was keeping both, which means he understood something that modern readers sometimes miss: that a story told in two radically different ways is not a story with an ambiguous identity. It is a story rich enough to survive multiple approaches without losing what it essentially is. The Atlakviða tells it at maximum compression and severity. The Atlamál tells it the way a tradition tells a story when it wants to let the grief show. Both are true to the material. The choice between them is a choice about what kind of attention you want to bring to bear, not about which version got it right.

Guðrún walks into the fire at the end of the Atlakviða. The poem does not follow her in. In the Atlamál she survives — or the poem ends before her death — and the survival is consistent with the larger arc of the tradition, which needs her alive for the final poems of the heroic cycle. The gold has done what the gold does. The curse has moved through Hreiðmarr, through Fáfnir, through Sigurðr, through the Gjukungs, through Atli, leaving nothing standing behind it and finding nothing yet to stop it. There is one more chapter in the reckoning, and it belongs to Guðrún's sons by a later marriage — sons who will ride out to avenge a sister they loved, in a poem that the tradition regards as the oldest voice in the entire corpus, and who will not come back.

Chapter 18

Hamðismál: The Oldest Voice

Start with what we know about this poem, then start over.

What we know: the Hamðismál is generally considered, on linguistic and stylistic grounds, to be among the oldest poems in the Poetic Edda. Its vocabulary is archaic even by Eddic standards, its syntax dense, its formulaic patterns reaching back toward a stage of the Germanic poetic tradition earlier than most of what the Codex Regius preserves. When scholars want to argue about the age of the corpus, the Hamðismál is usually one of their fixed points — a poem old enough that it connects the Norse tradition to a Germanic past that precedes, by centuries, the Icelandic manuscript culture that eventually wrote it down.

Now start over: the Hamðismál is a poem about two brothers who go to their deaths because one of them killed the brother who would have saved them, and everything else in the poem — the armor, the hall, the god who delivers the final blow — exists to make that fact land with its full weight.

The Situation

Guðrún has had more lives than the tradition usually permits a character. She has been Sigurðr's wife. She has been Atli's wife. She has survived both — survived Sigurðr's murder, survived her revenge on Atli, survived the burning hall, and washed up, eventually, in a third marriage to a king named Jónakr, with whom she has had three sons: Hamðir, Sörli, and Erpr.

She also has a daughter from an earlier marriage: Svanhildr, Sigurðr's daughter, who is famously the most beautiful woman in the world. Svanhildr has been given in marriage to Jörmunrekkr, king of the Goths — the historical Ermanaric, who died around 376 CE and whose legend the Germanic tradition preserved with the same process of mythological intensification it applied to Attila. Jörmunrekkr has had Svanhildr executed — trampled by horses — on the accusation of adultery with his own son, an accusation the tradition presents as manufactured and false.

Guðrún has one response available to her. She sends her sons to avenge their sister.

Before they leave, she gives them armor. The armor is magical — forged to be impervious to iron, which in the context of ninth or tenth-century weaponry means impervious to almost anything. Hamðir and Sörli cannot be killed by swords or spears or axes. They are, for the purposes of this battle, invulnerable — with one condition, which the poem holds back until the condition becomes the story's catastrophe.

Erpr

On the road to Jörmunrekkr's hall, the three brothers encounter Erpr — their half-brother, son of Jónakr by another woman. Erpr offers to help them. In the Norse tradition, an offer of help from a kinsman on a dangerous mission is not something you decline. What Hamðir asks, essentially, is: how much will you help? Erpr's answer is a kenning, a compressed image: he will help them the way a hand helps a foot, the way a foot helps a leg. He means he will be the essential connecting piece — the element that makes the whole system function, without which the other parts cannot do what they are designed to do.

Hamðir does not understand this, or does not choose to understand it. He interprets the answer as evasive — as offering nothing. He and Sörli kill Erpr on the road.

The kenning Erpr uses — hand to foot, foot to leg — is the kind of compressed metaphor the earlier chapter on Eddic technique examined. It requires the listener to assemble the meaning: a hand does not do the foot's work directly, but without the hand the system of the body is incomplete, and there are things the foot cannot do without the hand's contribution further up the chain. Erpr is saying he will be the third element in a three-part structure that only works when all three parts are present. He is saying this because he knows, and perhaps because he has been told, what the mission requires.

Whether the armor's magical protection extends fully to a two-man team or requires three is something the poem implies rather than states. The magic was made for three brothers. It may have been calibrated for three. Erpr's answer is not false modesty — it is an accurate description of a structural necessity, delivered in the only language available to him for describing it, and Hamðir's failure to parse that language is the error on which the entire poem turns.

The actual scene of the killing is brief — a few stanzas, a misunderstanding, a death. The weight comes from what follows, from the negative space that Erpr's absence creates in everything that comes after. He was going to help them the way a foot helps a leg. Without him, the system doesn't function. They will discover this when they reach the hall, and by then there will be nothing to do about it.

The Hall of Jörmunrekkr

What Hamðir and Sörli do at Jörmunrekkr's court is extraordinary. They cut off the king's hands and feet — the punishment that fits the crime of having Svanhildr trampled, a symmetry the tradition appreciated in its vengeance — and they do it while the king's bodyguard stands watching, unable to stop them. The magical armor works. Iron cannot touch them. They are moving through the hall like forces of nature, and for a moment it looks like they might actually complete what they came to do.

Then a man appears — grey-cloaked, one-eyed, the disguise so transparent to the reader that the poem barely bothers to maintain it. He speaks to Jörmunrekkr's men. He tells them: iron cannot kill these men. Use stones.

The grey-cloaked man is Odin. The poem does not name him, because it does not need to. He is the god who manages the battle-dead, who decides who falls and when, who has been moving through the heroic cycle in various disguises since its beginning. Here he intervenes not to save anyone but to ensure that the fated outcome occurs on schedule. Hamðir and Sörli cannot be killed by iron. Odin shows their enemies how to kill them anyway.

The intervention deserves more attention than it typically receives. Odin's appearance at the moment of the brothers' near-success is not anomalous in the heroic corpus — the god has been managing battle-fates throughout the tradition. What is distinctive here is the nakedness of it. He does not whisper tactics to a favorite warrior. He does not arrange a distraction or send a sign. He simply tells the enemy how to kill the men they cannot otherwise kill. Fate in the Völuspá is a cosmic architecture. Fate in the Hamðismál is Odin picking up a stone.

The stones find their marks. Before he dies, Hamðir says something that is the poem's most quoted passage and one of the most compressed philosophical statements in the corpus: we have fought well, we stand on Gothic corpses, we have achieved what we came to achieve — the king is maimed as he required — and we would be standing over his dead body too if Erpr had lived. The sentence that ends with Erpr's name is the sentence the poem has been building toward since the road. It is spoken without self-pity, without recrimination, almost as a piece of information: here is what happened, here is what was missing, here is the gap where the outcome should have been.

Sörli adds something equally precise: they have fought against giants of men and found their way to the end of the battle. No consolation, no illusion. Just the statement of what was done, and then the stones.

The Irony That Holds the Poem Together

The Hamðismál is structurally built on irony — not the rhetorical device, but the condition of knowing too late what you needed to know earlier.

Hamðir kills Erpr in a moment of anger or contempt or genuine misunderstanding — the poem does not specify which, and the ambiguity is almost certainly deliberate. The three possible readings produce three different moral tonalities. If Hamðir misunderstood the kenning, the tragedy is cognitive — a failure of comprehension that kills a man and ensures the mission's failure. If Hamðir understood but chose contempt, the tragedy is pride, the heroic virtue shading into the fatal flaw. If Hamðir simply did not want to share the glory of the revenge, the tragedy is something more complicated and less forgivable.

All three readings remain available. What the poem does not leave available is the possibility that Hamðir's error was minor or that its consequences were anything but total. Erpr's death is the wrong act at the wrong moment, and the wrongness reverberates through everything that follows. The armor that makes them invulnerable to iron is useless against stones, and they would have known this if the third piece of the system had been intact. The hand that helps the foot is the piece they discarded on the road, and they do not understand what they have discarded until the moment they are about to be crushed by boulders.

Guðrún's End

The poem's framing device places Guðrún at its opening, sending her sons away, and then returns to her at intervals in the memory of what she has lost. She has been losing things since Sigurðr died, and each loss has been named and recorded in the Völsung cycle's extraordinary succession of laments and elegies. By the time the Hamðismál opens, she is a woman who has been defined by loss for longer than many people live.

She does not appear in the hall of Jörmunrekkr. She does not witness what her sons achieve or how they die. She sends them out and the poem moves with them, and she waits in the same position she has occupied since the beginning of her story: the one who survives, who endures, who outlasts everyone she loved.

The Hamðismál does not give her a final lament. It ends with her sons' deaths and the simple absence of what might have been, and Guðrún is somewhere behind the poem's frame, having sent away the last thing she had to send. Her silence at the poem's end is the most eloquent silence in the corpus — more eloquent than the weeping over Sigurðr's body, more eloquent than the laments she has already delivered. She has already said everything there is to say. The poem knows this and does not ask her to say it again.

The Oldest Voice and What It Tells Us

The Hamðismál's antiquity matters beyond its philological interest. A poem this old, preserved this intact, connected to historical events of the fifth century and encoded in a poetic language that predates the Viking Age, is evidence that the Norse heroic tradition was not invented in Iceland. It was carried there — from Norway, from an older Germanic world, from a tradition of sung poetry that ran from the Migration Period through the Viking Age and into the literate culture that eventually wrote it down.

The connection to Jordanes is worth dwelling on briefly. The Getica, written around 551 CE, describes the Gothic king Ermanaric executing a woman named Sunilda by having her torn apart by horses — the same punishment Svanhildr receives in the Norse tradition — and her brothers Sarus and Ammius wounding him in revenge. The names are different, the details vary, but the structural skeleton is identical across two traditions that diverged centuries before either text was written down. This is the deep time of the Germanic heroic tradition: stories that predate both their written sources, carried orally across the migrations, surviving in two literary traditions simultaneously as evidence of a common origin.

What the Hamðismál carries from that older world is its sensibility more than its plot: the specific combination of fatalism and agency, the willingness to proceed toward a known catastrophe without self-deception, the insistence that what matters is not the outcome but the quality of the action that produces it.

Hamðir and Sörli fail. They fail because of a mistake made in anger on a road, which is a very small and very human kind of failure. The armor held. The swords found their marks. The king paid the price that was required. The thing that didn't work was a relationship — a piece of kinship, discarded before its value was understood.

One more thing deserves attention before we leave this poem. It is the only poem in the heroic corpus that ends with a statement of conditional success — we would have done it, if. Every other heroic poem ends in failure or in the silence after failure. The Hamðismál ends with a hero assessing his own failure with complete accuracy and complete equanimity, identifying the specific, fixable, unfixed mistake that produced it. The final lines are not a lament. They are a report.

This is the oldest voice in the corpus telling us, at the tradition's end, that the heroic ideal does not require self-deception. You can know where you went wrong and still have fought as well as you could with what you had. The two things coexist without contradiction. Hamðir dies holding that knowledge without softening it, which is as good an ending as this tradition knows how to give.

The Poetic Edda's heroic section ends here — not with triumph, not with a death that redeems everything before it, but with two brothers under a pile of stones in a Gothic king's hall, one of them saying: we would have done it, if the third had lived.

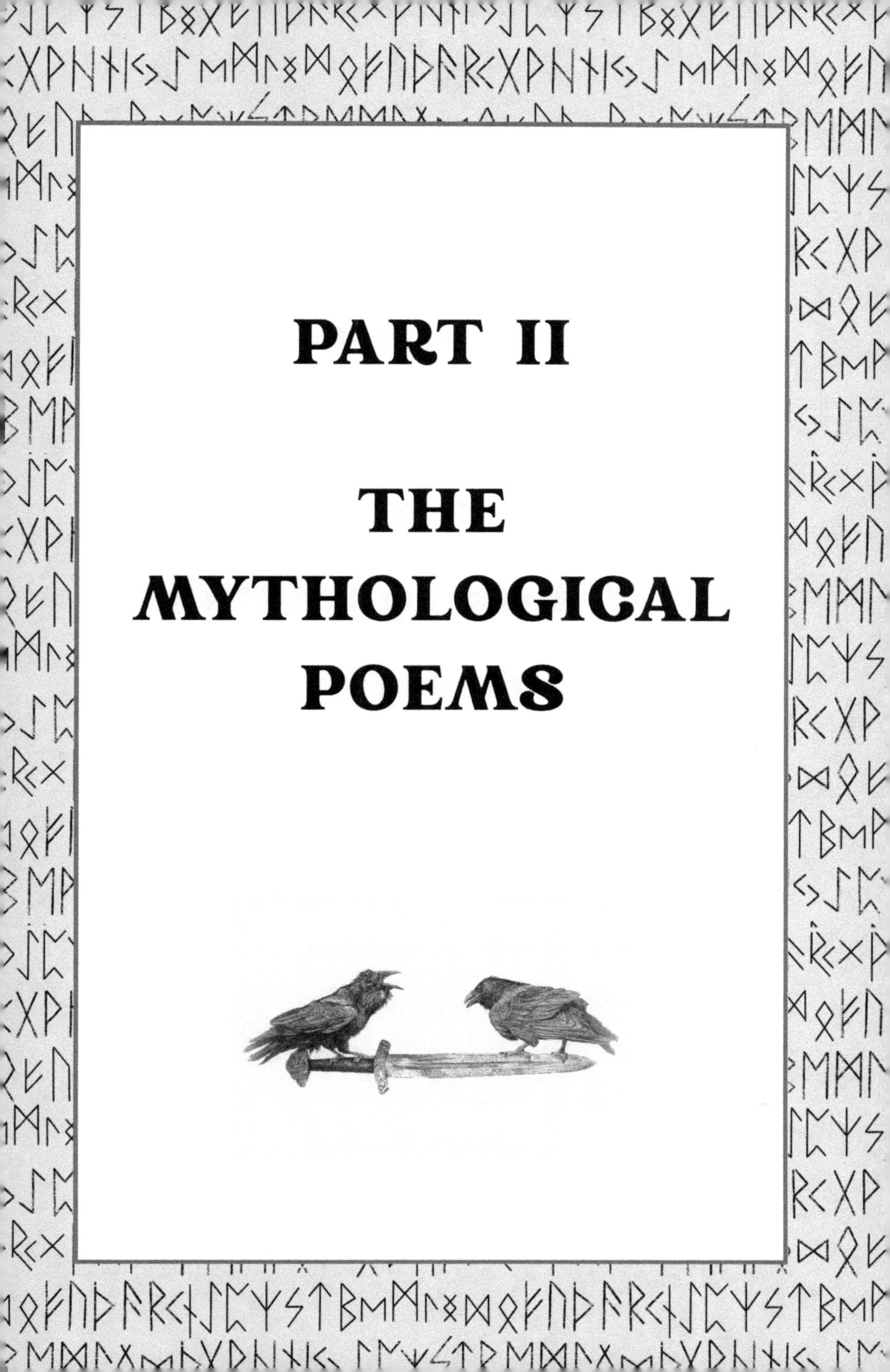

PART II

THE MYTHOLOGICAL POEMS

Chapter 19

The Poetic Edda and Modern Asatru Practice

The question comes up regularly in Asatru communities, and it never gets a clean answer: to what extent can a thirteenth-century manuscript be a living spiritual document?

The people asking are not being difficult. They are grappling with something genuinely complicated — the relationship between textual preservation and religious authenticity, between historical distance and present-tense meaning, between the scholar's careful handling of a fragile source and the practitioner's need for something to hold onto on a Tuesday morning when things are going badly. The Poetic Edda is the closest thing the modern Norse religious revival has to a primary scripture. It is also a collection of anonymous poems composed over several centuries, written down by Christian scribes, preserved through a series of accidents, and interpreted by every generation that has encountered it according to that generation's own needs and blind spots.

Both of these things are true simultaneously, and the practice of modern Asatru lives in the tension between them.

What Asatru Is and Isn't

Before examining how the Poetic Edda functions within Asatru, a brief orientation helps — because Asatru is not a unified religion with a central authority, a fixed creed, or a canonical set of practices, and that diversity shapes how any text functions within it.

Asatru — the name derives from Old Norse Ása trú, "faith in the Æsir" — is the broad term for the modern revival of Norse paganism, which emerged in Iceland and Scandinavia in the early 1970s and has since spread across Europe, North America, and beyond. Different communities approach it differently: some are strictly reconstructionist, working to reproduce pre-Christian Norse practice as accurately as the evidence allows; others are more eclectic, drawing on the textual tradition for inspiration while adapting practice to contemporary circumstances; others still treat Asatru primarily as a philosophical or ethical framework rather than a theistic religion in the conventional sense.

What virtually all of these approaches share is the Poetic Edda. It is the common ground, the reference point to which every practitioner returns, the text that more than any other defines what it means to engage with the Norse tradition seriously. This makes it something quite different from what it was when the Codex Regius was compiled: not a repository of mythological material for antiquarian preservation, not a sourcebook for skaldic poetry, but a living document in active use by people who derive genuine meaning from it.

That transformation — from manuscript to scripture — is not without complications, and the complications are worth naming honestly.

The Völuspá in Ritual Context

In practice, the Völuspá is the Poetic Edda's most liturgically active text. This is partly because of its cosmological scope — it covers the whole arc of the Norse universe in a single poem, which makes it useful as an overture for any ritual occasion — and partly because its spoken register, the incantatory ljóðaháttr meter with its short, weighted lines, translates into ritual performance more naturally than the driving fornyrðislag of the heroic poems. When the Völuspá is read aloud in a ritual space, the meter does work that it also does in its original context: it slows the listener down, creates a quality of attention different from ordinary speech, and produces the slight disorientation of entering a different register of language that is characteristic of effective liturgy in many traditions.

It is recited at blót — the seasonal ritual that marks the major points of the Norse calendar, including the solstices, equinoxes, and the festivals of Dísablót, Sigrblót, and Winternights. The recitation is not typically the whole poem — sixty-six stanzas would require more time than most ritual contexts accommodate — but selected passages, particularly the cosmogonic opening and the Ragnarök sequence, serve as framing texts for the ritual's central acts of offering and invocation. The blót itself varies considerably between communities. Some conduct it with elaborate liturgical structure; others with a minimal framework that leaves space for spontaneous speech and offering. Across these variations, what remains consistent is the use of the Völuspá as a cosmological anchor — the text that establishes the frame before anything else happens. Communities that have been practicing for decades report a cumulative effect: the cosmology begins to feel inhabited rather than theoretical, the gods begin to feel present rather than historical, and the words of the seeress begin to carry the weight of a tradition rather than just a manuscript.

The sumbel — the formal drinking ritual in which participants make toasts, oaths, and boasts in sequence around the horn — uses the Völuspá differently: as a source of invocations, specific verses addressed to specific gods to open or close the ritual, quotations embedded in the spoken parts of the ceremony to ground them in the textual tradition. In this use the poem functions less as liturgy and more as a shared language — a set of references that practitioners can invoke in the confidence that other practitioners will recognize them.

The Hávamál as Ethical Code

If the Völuspá is the Poetic Edda's liturgical text, the Hávamál is its ethical one.

In modern Asatru, the Hávamál has generated the most sustained engagement of any Eddic poem because its concerns are the most immediately practical. The questions it addresses — how to conduct yourself in the world, how to maintain relationships that hold, what wisdom costs and why it is worth the cost — are questions practitioners ask themselves outside of ritual contexts, in the ordinary run of their lives.

The most influential and most controversial attempt to systematize the Hávamál's ethics for modern practice is the Nine Noble Virtues — a list of values (courage, truth, honor, fidelity, discipline, hospitality, self-reliance, industriousness, perseverance) derived primarily from the Hávamál and promoted as a practical ethical framework. The Nine Noble Virtues were formalized in the 1970s by the Odinic Rite, one of the earliest Asatru organizations, and have since become the most widely recognized ethical statement in the tradition — and the most widely debated.

The debate is instructive. Critics argue that the Nine Noble Virtues are a post-hoc systematization that imposes a coherence the Hávamál does not actually have — that the poem's ethics are more situational, more contextual, more contradictory than any tidy list can represent. They argue that the list selects certain values while ignoring others equally prominent: cunning, for instance, which the Hávamál treats as a survival skill rather than a moral failing, and which appears nowhere in the Nine Noble Virtues. Defenders argue that every religious tradition requires some distillation of its ethics into memorable and teachable form, and that the list is useful because it is memorable and gives practitioners something to hold in mind during ordinary situations.

Both sides are partially right. The Nine Noble Virtues are a useful entry point into the Hávamál's ethics for newcomers, and an inadequate representation of those ethics for anyone who engages with the poem seriously. The appropriate response is not to abandon the list but to read past it — to treat the Nine Noble Virtues as a door into the Hávamál rather than a substitute for it.

The Sigrdrífumál as Runic Text

The Sigrdrífumál occupies a specific and important place in the practice of runology — the study and use of the runic tradition for magical and contemplative purposes.

The poem is the primary Eddic source for runic application: its catalogue of victory runes, birth runes, wave runes, healing runes, and thought runes constitutes the most detailed account in the corpus of how runes were understood to function in practice. Practitioners engaged with the runic tradition use the Sigrdrífumál as a reference point and a source of inspiration — not as a complete manual, but as evidence that the tradition understood runes as operational rather than merely symbolic, as tools for specific purposes in specific contexts.

The relationship between the Sigrdrífumál and the Rúnatal in the Hávamál is one that practitioners navigate constantly: the first gives the application, the second gives the myth of origin, and together they form a two-part framework for understanding what the runes are and what they do. The Rúnatal's account of Odin's sacrifice provides the theological and psychological ground for the Sigrdrífumál's practical catalogue. You can use the Sigrdrífumál without engaging with the Rúnatal, but the practice will be shallower for it.

This connection between the two texts illustrates something important about how the corpus functions for practitioners: not as a collection of independent texts but as a network of cross-references, where the full meaning of any one poem is enriched by its relationships to the others.

The Problem of Authenticity

Every practitioner in the modern Asatru tradition eventually confronts the same question: how authentic is what we are doing? And behind that question, usually unspoken but always present: does it matter?

The two questions need to be separated. Whether a given practice is historically accurate is a question with an empirical answer, even if that answer is often "we don't know." Whether historical accuracy is the right criterion for evaluating a practice is a philosophical question with no empirical answer, and different practitioners answer it differently.

The reconstructionist position — that we should work to recover historical practice as accurately as possible — produces careful scholarship and genuine historical depth. It also produces, sometimes, a paralysis in the face of gaps in the evidence that are simply too large to bridge. The living tradition position — that the tradition should be allowed to grow and adapt in response to contemporary circumstances, as all living religious traditions do — produces vitality and relevance. It also produces, sometimes, a looseness with the historical material that strips it of the specific density that makes it worth engaging with in the first place.

The most thoughtful voices in the modern Asatru community have reached a position that this book endorses: the Poetic Edda should be treated as a living source rather than a dead text. Not every word in it is equally applicable to contemporary practice. Not every value it embodies is worth embracing uncritically. But the cosmological vision, the ethical framework, the specific kind of dignity under pressure that the corpus models again and again — these are not museum artifacts. They are resources, available to anyone willing to do the work of understanding them.

Connecting the Texts

This book is part of a series, and the Poetic Edda is the series' deepest layer — the source behind the source behind the source. The Prose Edda drew on it. The runic tradition is encoded in it. The stories that Norse mythology tells about the gods, the cosmos, and the human condition are here in their oldest recoverable form, before Snorri smoothed them for a Christian audience, before the later tradition had time to develop the theological apparatus that sometimes obscures what the original was doing.

At its best, what the original was doing is what the best religious literature always does: providing a framework within which human experience becomes legible. The suffering that produces knowledge. The love that crosses the boundary of death. The courage that acts in the full awareness of futility. The community that holds together through the maintenance of specific obligations toward specific people. The world that ends and begins again, not because someone arranged it that way, but because that is the nature of things.

The Poetic Edda does not make these themes easy. It does not resolve them into comfort or into simple instruction. It holds them in the tension that is their natural state and asks the reader to sit with that tension — which is the hardest and most necessary thing a text can ask. The poems are the map. The practice is the walking.

Chapter 20

Themes That Speak to Us Now

Open the Poetic Edda at random and you will land somewhere in the vicinity of a thousand years ago — a world of kings and giants and gods who die, of women who weave fate and men who know they are going to lose and fight anyway. The surface is remote, but the concerns beneath the surface are not.

This chapter is a deliberate slowing down — a step back from the poem-by-poem analysis of the previous sections to ask what the corpus as a whole is saying about things that have not changed. Not what it meant to its original audience, but what it means now, read by people who do not believe in Odin and may never have heard of örlög, but who recognize, in poem after poem, something that is happening to them or has happened to them or will happen to them before they are done.

The themes are not separate. They are a web, each one pulling on the others. But they can be approached one at a time.

Fate and Freedom: The Dignity of Acting Anyway

What the Norse corpus demands of its reader philosophically is also what contemporary life most urgently requires.

The gods know they will lose at Ragnarök. They know this in the specific, detailed way of people who have been told the names of their killers and the manner of their deaths. Odin knows Fenrir will swallow him. Thor knows the serpent's venom will take him nine steps after he kills it. Freyr knows he will face Surtr without the sword he gave away for love. They act in the full possession of this knowledge and they do not change their behavior because of it. They maintain their alliances, they pursue their purposes, they laugh at Ægir's table and send their ravens out in the morning. They live as if the knowledge of their deaths changes nothing about the living — which is not denial, not pretending it won't happen, but something harder and more interesting: the decision that how you move through time is not determined by how it ends.

The Stoics of antiquity reached a similar position from a different direction — the distinction between what is up to us and what is not, the insistence on acting with full virtue regardless of external outcomes, the equanimity in the face of what cannot be controlled. But the Norse version is starker, because the Stoic framework retains the assurance of a rational cosmic order in which right action is ultimately aligned with how things are. That assurance is absent here. The gods act well and still lose. The heroes maintain their integrity and still die badly. The alignment between virtue and outcome is not guaranteed by the structure of the universe, and the corpus does not pretend otherwise. The action is right anyway — not because the outcome might change, but because the action is where meaning lives.

Fatalism is something different: the shrug, the refusal to act because the outcome is predetermined. The position these poems model is its opposite — act fully, with complete awareness of what the outcome will be, because the action itself is the point. The Völuspá does not say the gods fight at Ragnarök because they think they can win. It says they fight because they are the gods, and this is what the gods do, and the fact that it ends in fire does not alter what they are while it is happening.

The contemporary relevance of this is not obscure. Every serious engagement with climate change, with political injustice, with chronic illness, with any form of long-term struggle against a force that may not be beatable on the timeline available, involves a version of the same question: how do you act with full commitment when full commitment may not be enough? The corpus's answer is not comforting, but it is serious: you act because that is what you are, and what you are is not determined by what you achieve.

The Cost of Knowledge

Every piece of genuine understanding Odin acquires costs him something real. His eye at Mímir's well. Nine nights on the World Tree for the runes. Huginn and Muninn sent out every morning knowing they may not return, and when they do return, what they bring him is more knowledge of a world that is going to end. The pattern is consistent across the entire mythology: the cost is not incidental, not a price paid separately from the knowledge itself. It is constitutive — the suffering is part of how the knowledge is acquired. You cannot have Odin's wisdom without Odin's wounds.

This sits in tension with modernity's preferred model of knowledge acquisition, which tends toward the frictionless — the Google search, the Wikipedia article, the podcast that summarizes a book in forty-five minutes. The Hávamál's gnomic wisdom is deeply practical and designed for immediate application. But it insists, at a deeper level, that the knowledge which changes you — the knowledge that matters most — does not come without a cost proportional to its importance.

Outside of myth, this looks like the understanding of grief that you cannot acquire except by grieving. The comprehension of courage that requires having been afraid and having acted anyway. The wisdom about relationships that accumulates only through the specific education of having relationships fail. The gods and heroes carry this kind of knowledge — not information but formation, understanding pressed into the shape of a person by the weight of experience. Odin on the World Tree is not learning about suffering. He is becoming someone who has suffered enough to understand what suffering accesses.

The tradition's most uncomfortable implication is that the shortcuts don't work — that wisdom of the kind that matters is not transferable by summary, not available in advance of the experience that produces it, and not separable from the damage the experience leaves behind. The runes are carved in the body, not stored in a file.

Grief and Its Work

The Poetic Edda contains more sustained attention to grief than any other body of ancient literature I am aware of, and it handles grief with a specificity that most traditions cannot match.

The Guðrúnarkviður give us grief in stages: the shock that cannot weep, the hand on the dead face that finally permits tears, the retrospective accounting of losses so comprehensive that the telling of them is itself a form of mourning. The Helgi poems give us grief that refuses the boundary of death — love persistent enough to pull a dead man back to the burial mound for one night, and the second grief of waiting for him after that and receiving nothing. The Helreið Brynhildar gives us grief that has been converted into testimony — the insistence on the accurate record as a form of posthumous dignity. The heroic laments give us grief as the precondition for revenge, which is itself a form of grief, a way of carrying a loss through action when mourning alone is not sufficient to contain it.

Old Norse has a richer vocabulary for grief than English does. Harmr covers distress and sorrow; sút conveys anxiety and grief combined; tregr is the specific heaviness of accumulated loss. The heroic poems move between these registers — acute grief at the moment of loss, chronic grief as a condition of survival, grief that has been metabolized into action without being resolved. Guðrún's trajectory through the corpus is in part a study in all three: the acute grief of the first Guðrúnarkviða, the chronic grief of the second and third lays, and the acted grief of the Atlakviða, where what she feels has become what she does.

What the corpus does with grief that is unusual is refuse to resolve it. These poems do not offer consolation in the sense of a promise that the loss will be redeemed or that the dead are in a better place or that the grief will pass. They offer instead the legitimacy of the grief itself — the insistence that what you are feeling is commensurate with what you have lost, that the magnitude of the response is not disproportionate but accurate, that grief of this size requires this much space.

The Hávamál is unusually direct on one specific aspect of grief: do not keep your sorrow locked up so long that it becomes toxic — speak it to a trusted person, because unspeakable grief is a burden that increases in the carrying. This is the poem's most psychologically sophisticated observation, and it sits in productive tension with its advice about not advertising vulnerability. The corpus understood that grief requires both containment and expression — that the person who never shows their grief is carrying something that will eventually break them, and the person who shows it indiscriminately is handing power to people who will use it. The wisdom is in the calibration: grief expressed to the right person at the right moment, neither suppressed into toxicity nor broadcast into vulnerability.

The counter-intuitive teaching runs through the entire corpus: that the appropriate response to significant loss is not to get over it but to take it in, fully, and become the person who has had that specific experience. The difference between containing grief and denying it matters enormously here, and the corpus holds strongly to the former while rejecting the latter.

Violence and What It Means to Read It

The Poetic Edda is a violent text, and this needs to be said plainly — not as a warning or an apology, but as a fact that requires honest engagement rather than either discomfort or defensiveness.

The heroic poems describe decapitation, mutilation, the killing of children, the serving of flesh at a feast, the blinding of enemies, the breaking of bodies in battle. The mythological poems describe the torture of Loki, the burning of Gullveig, the mutilation of Týr. The violence is not incidental to the narrative — in many cases it is the narrative, the precise form that the poems' concerns take when they are made concrete.

The question of how to read this in the twenty-first century has more than one legitimate answer, and part of the task is resisting the temptation to reach for just one of them. The first answer is that the violence in the Poetic Edda is not gratuitous. It is the language in which certain kinds of meaning are expressed in this tradition. The killing of children in the Atlakviða is not a representation of child-killing as something desirable. It is the extreme expression of a specific kind of grief and a specific kind of vengeance, taken to the furthest possible point to show what total loss produces in a person who has already lost everything. The violence is the measure of what preceded it.

The second answer is to take seriously the question of why these texts have lasted. Texts that are merely violent do not last — they are forgotten when the cultural moment that produced them passes. The Poetic Edda has lasted for a thousand years because the violence is in service of something that is not violent: the questions about fate, identity, love, loss, and what it means to live with full awareness of your own mortality. The violence is the form. The content is everything this chapter has been discussing.

The third answer — and this is harder — is to hold the text's violence in honest tension with the question of what it models and endorses. The Skírnismál's curse sequence is a detailed account of psychological coercion. The Atlakviða's revenge is the killing of children by their mother. The reader who engages with these texts without sitting with that discomfort is not reading them fully. The tradition's willingness to show the full cost of its own values is one of its most serious qualities, and it deserves a serious response.

The Feminine in the Poetic Edda

An honest assessment of women in the Poetic Edda requires holding two things simultaneously: the tradition gives women more agency, more interiority, and more narrative weight than most comparable bodies of ancient literature — and it also produces the Skírnismál, where a woman is coerced into marriage by magical torture, and the Völundarkviða, where a woman is raped in a scene the poem narrates without moral comment.

Both are true. The tradition that gives us Sigrún choosing her warrior, Brynhildr delivering her last testimony, Guðrún surviving everything and becoming something terrible and magnificent — this is the same tradition that gives us Gerðr and Böðvildr as objects of male will, used by the narrative and then set aside. The corpus is not consistent on this. Neither is any other tradition of comparable antiquity, and this one is considerably more willing than most to give its female characters genuine interiority and genuine agency even within patriarchal structures it never questions.

The valkyries are the tradition's most distinctive contribution to the representation of female power: women who move between worlds, who choose which warriors live and which die, who select their own lovers, who defy the gods when their loyalties require it and pay the price of that defiance without self-pity. Sigrún, Brynhildr,

Sigrdrífa are agents, making choices that carry full weight in the narratives they inhabit. The völur represent a different kind of female power — not physical or political but epistemic. The völva who opens the Völuspá knows more than Odin. She knows more than everyone. The nornir who weave fate at the base of Yggdrasill do not operate within the divine order. They constitute it. The women who see clearly in this tradition are its source, not its periphery.

The corpus's best offering to contemporary readers thinking about gender is a clear-eyed presentation of female knowledge, female choice, and female consequence as fully serious matters — as important as anything the male characters do, and sometimes more so. The Norse world did not practice equality, and the texts do not pretend it did. What they offer instead is something rarer: the consistent treatment of women's inner lives as worthy of the same narrative weight as men's.

Chapter 21

The Edda in the Modern World

In 1937, J.R.R. Tolkien gave a lecture at Oxford called "Beowulf: The Monsters and the Critics" that changed how scholars thought about Old English poetry. He argued, against the prevailing academic consensus, that the monsters in Beowulf were not an embarrassment to an otherwise serious text but were the point — that the poem was a meditation on mortality, on the relationship between human courage and cosmic darkness, and that the monsters embodied that darkness in the only adequate form available to the tradition that produced them.

He was describing the Norse mythological corpus at the same time. Tolkien spent years inside the Eddic poems — reading them, translating them, lecturing on them, and absorbing them so thoroughly that they became part of the imaginative substrate from which his own mythology grew. The debt is not hidden. The names of the dwarves in The Hobbit — Thorin, Fíli, Kíli, Óin, Glóin, Dwalin, Balin, Bifur, Bofur, Bombur, Nori, Dori, Ori — come almost wholesale from the Völuspá's catalogue of dwarf names in the stanzas describing the creation of the first beings. Gandalf's name is in the same list. The wandering wizard with the broad-brimmed hat and the staff, who turns up at unexpected moments and whose advice is cryptic and whose purposes are larger than they appear, is Odin. Not an Odin-inspired character. Odin, translated into the specific register of a children's book that was always more than a children's book.

What Tolkien took from the corpus was not decoration but architecture. The Norse understanding of eucatastrophe — the turn at the end of the Völuspá, the new earth rising from the sea after Ragnarök — gave him the structural principle he needed to write his own mythology's endings. He wanted the consolation of renewal without the requirement of Christian eschatology. The corpus provided it, in a form ancient enough to carry weight and flexible enough to accommodate his own theological commitments. The result is the most successful single transmission of the Norse mythological sensibility into a popular modern form — more successful, arguably, than any explicit retelling, because Tolkien did not retell the Norse myths. He wrote from inside them.

The influence runs deeper than nomenclature. The structure of Tolkien's mythology — a world that was made perfect and has been falling toward a final catastrophe ever since, in which the forces of good fight knowing they cannot ultimately win, in which the measure of a character is what they do in the face of certain defeat — is the Norse cosmological vision translated into a different idiom. He wanted the Völuspá's renewal after Ragnarök, but he wanted it to mean more than the Norse tradition required it to mean.

Neil Gaiman and the Limits of Narrative

Neil Gaiman's Norse Mythology, published in 2017, is the most widely read contemporary engagement with the material this book covers. It is beautifully written, genuinely affectionate toward its sources, and extremely good at doing what it sets out to do: making the Norse gods accessible to contemporary readers who might find the Eddas themselves forbidding.

It is also, necessarily, a translation in the deepest sense — not just from Old Norse to English, but from poem to prose, from the fragmentary and allusive to the continuous and explained, from texts that trust their readers with gaps to a narrative that fills the gaps in because narrative requires filling them. Gaiman's instincts about which details matter are generally sound, and his versions of Odin and Thor and Loki are recognizable from the tradition. But the Poetic Edda's great silences — the moments where the compression is the technique, where what is left out is as powerful as what is said — cannot survive the translation into storytelling prose. A story that explains itself is a different thing from a poem that doesn't.

This is an observation about the nature of the project rather than a criticism of Gaiman's book, which is excellent at what it is. Popularization requires smoothing, and the Poetic Edda's roughness — its archaic density, its ellipses, its presupposed knowledge — is not separable from its power. What Gaiman gives readers is a door. The people who walk through it and find their way to the Poetic Edda itself — who discover that the sources are stranger and more demanding and more alive than the retelling — will have Gaiman to thank for the introduction. The room on the other side is different from the door, but you need the door to find the room.

Marvel and the Uses of Mythology

The Marvel Cinematic Universe's Thor and Loki bear roughly the relationship to the Eddic tradition that a photograph of a landscape bears to the landscape itself — recognizable, useful for some purposes, and fundamentally different in kind from the thing it represents.

Mythology has always traveled through popular culture, accumulating new forms without losing its older ones. The gods of Greece became the gods of Rome became the allegorical figures of the Renaissance became the psychological archetypes of the twentieth century, and the Olympians are still there, in the Iliad, for anyone who wants them. The Marvel Thor is not the end of the Eddic Thor. He is one of Thor's current cultural addresses, and the people who arrive at the Poetic Edda through Marvel are doing something the tradition has always accommodated: following a thread from a popular form back toward its source.

What the Marvel versions cannot provide — and do not try to — is the cosmological weight that makes the original figures worth engaging with seriously. The Marvel Loki is a compelling villain-hero whose complexity is largely psychological: family dynamics, identity, the desire for recognition. The Eddic Loki is all of that and also a philosophical position — the chaos necessary to the system's functioning, the truth-teller whose truths are also weapons, the outsider whose exclusion guarantees the disaster that his inclusion also guaranteed. They share a name and some surface characteristics, and the overlap more or less ends there.

The same applies to Thor. The Eddic Thor is not charming or glamorous. He is reliable, direct, occasionally ridiculous, completely indispensable. His heroism is not the heroism of the individual genius — it is the heroism of the one who shows up, consistently, with the right tool, and does what needs to be done without requiring it to be elegant. Marvel has made him beautiful and occasionally witty. The tradition made him necessary — and the gap between those two things is instructive about what each culture values.

Wagner and the Danger of Transformation

The most influential and most dangerous engagement with the Norse mythological tradition in the modern period is Richard Wagner's Der Ring des Nibelungen — four operas composed between 1848 and 1874, spanning roughly sixteen hours of music, representing the most ambitious artistic response to the Völsung cycle that has ever been attempted.

Wagner was not working primarily from the Eddic poems. He was working from the Völsunga saga, the thirteenth-century prose compilation that draws heavily on the Eddic sources, and from the Nibelungenlied. His Ring is therefore already a transformation of a transformation. But its power — musical, theatrical, philosophical — is such that for many people in the nineteenth and early twentieth centuries it became the definitive version of the material, displacing the sources it drew from in the popular imagination.

The problem this created is historical and still live. Wagner's nationalism, his antisemitism, and his use of Germanic mythology as the foundation for a specifically German cultural identity made the Ring cycle available for appropriation by the cultural politics that culminated in National Socialism. The Nazis did not need to misread Wagner — they read him accurately enough, in at least this respect. And the association between Norse mythology and German nationalist ideology, cemented by Wagner and weaponized by the Nazi cultural apparatus, created a shadow that the tradition has not fully escaped.

This matters for anyone engaging seriously with the Poetic Edda today: the tradition has been used for purposes that are antithetical to the values most of its contemporary readers and practitioners hold, and that use cannot simply be disavowed and moved past. It requires a direct confrontation with the question of what it means to reclaim material that has been contaminated by association with ideologies of racial hierarchy and ethnic exclusion.

The answer that the Asatru community has been developing, slowly and with considerable internal debate, is the right one in outline: the Norse mythological tradition is not the property of any ethnic or national group, does not encode racial hierarchy in its original form, and has been practiced historically by people of considerable ethnic and cultural diversity. The gods of the Poetic Edda are not Germanic nationalist symbols. They are figures from a specific pre-Christian religious tradition that happen to have been claimed, fraudulently, for nationalist purposes. Reclaiming them requires naming the fraud explicitly and maintaining the distinction between the tradition and its misuse. That work is uncomfortable. It is also necessary, and the poems are worth it.

Why the Poems Last

The Codex Regius is in Reykjavik, in a climate-controlled case in the Árni Magnússon Institute for Icelandic Studies. It is about the size of a paperback. It is made of calfskin. It has a gap in the middle where eight pages are missing, and nobody knows why or when they were removed. It was written down around 1270, compiled from sources that were already old, preserving poems that had been traveling in oral tradition for centuries before that.

Right now, someone needs it.

The poems have survived bad readings — readings that stripped them of their complexity to make them serve a political agenda, readings that romanticized them into Nordic escapism, readings that reduced their gods to cartoon warriors and their cosmology to a video game aesthetic. None of these readings killed the poems. They absorbed them, the way they absorbed the Christian scribes who wrote them down, and they continue to exist in their original form, available to anyone willing to approach them on their own terms.

Their durability is not a matter of age or aesthetic achievement or importance to the history of European literature, though they have all of these things. Their durability is their continued usefulness. People keep returning to them because they keep finding something that couldn't be found elsewhere — a way of holding the knowledge of their own mortality without being flattened by it, a framework for understanding loss that doesn't promise resolution, a vision of courage that doesn't require a guarantee of success.

The völva raised from the dead by Odin sees everything — the void before creation, the age of gold, the wars of the gods, the presages of catastrophe, the catastrophe itself, the silence after it, the new green earth that rises from the sea when the silence lifts. She speaks without consolation and without evasion. She descends when she is done. The poem does not follow her.

That ending — the descent, the silence, the world continuing without her — is the Poetic Edda's final image of itself. Voices from a long time ago, speaking things that were old when they were first spoken, written down by people who knew they were preserving something that could not otherwise survive, passed through every form of misreading and misappropriation available to a text over seven centuries. Still here. Still doing what they were made to do.

The gap in the middle of the Codex Regius is permanent. Eight pages are gone. What remains is still the most significant body of mythological poetry in the Germanic tradition, still the deepest source we have for a specific way of understanding what it means to be alive in a world that will end. Read them. They have always been enough.

Appendix A — Glossary of Key Characters and Beings

A reference guide to the principal figures encountered in this book. Entries are alphabetical by the most common English rendering of the name. Old Norse forms appear in parentheses where they differ significantly. This is not an exhaustive catalogue of the Norse mythological tradition — it is a working tool for readers who need quick orientation while reading.

Andvari. A dwarf who lives in a waterfall in the shape of a pike, possessor of a vast gold hoard including the ring Andvaranaut. Caught by Loki, who forces him to surrender his treasure as blood-payment. Andvari curses the gold as it is taken from him, setting in motion the chain of destruction that drives the Völsung cycle.

Atli (*Atli Buðlason*). King of the Huns, husband of Guðrún after Sigurðr's death. Lures Guðrún's brothers Gunnarr and Högni to his court with promises of gold, kills them, and is in turn destroyed by Guðrún's revenge. The Norse tradition's version of the historical Attila the Hun.

Baldr. Son of Odin and Frigg, described as the most beloved and most beautiful of the gods. His death — engineered by Loki, executed unwittingly by the blind god Höðr — marks the beginning of the end for the divine order. Returns after Ragnarök in the renewed world.

Brynhildr. Valkyrie, warrior-woman, the most complex figure in the Völsung cycle. Put to sleep by Odin on the mountain Hindarfjall as punishment for defying his will in battle. Woken by Sigurðr, to whom she pledges herself, then separated from him by Grímhildr's forgetting-potion and a series of deceptions. Engineers Sigurðr's death and dies on his funeral pyre. Her final monologue, delivered in the *Helreið Brynhildar*, is among the most powerful passages in the corpus.

Fáfnir. Originally a dwarf, brother of Reginn. Transformed himself into a dragon to guard the gold he stole from his father Hreiðmarr. Killed by Sigurðr, whose dialogue with the dying dragon is one of the Poetic Edda's most philosophically striking exchanges. His blood, accidentally tasted by Sigurðr, gives the hero the ability to understand the language of birds.

Fenrir (*Fenrisúlfr*). The great wolf, son of Loki and the giantess Angrboða. Bound by the gods with the magical fetter Gleipnir after growing too large to be safely contained. At Ragnarök he breaks free and swallows Odin. Killed by Víðarr in revenge.

Freyr. Vanir god of fertility, sunshine, and the growing season. Son of Njörðr, twin of Freyja. Gives away his magical self-fighting sword to obtain the giantess Gerðr as his wife, an act that leaves him unarmed at Ragnarök. His desire for Gerðr is the subject of the *Skírnismál.*

Freyja. Vanir goddess of love, desire, fertility, and seiðr magic. Twin of Freyr, daughter of Njörðr. Owner of the Brísingamen necklace and the falcon-cloak. Receives half the battle-dead in her hall Fólkvangr. One of the tradition's most powerful divine figures, whose sexuality is a form of authority rather than vulnerability.

Frigg. Odin's wife, queen of the Æsir, mother of Baldr. Attempted to protect Baldr by extracting oaths from everything in existence not to harm him. Her failure to obtain an oath from the mistletoe enables Loki's plot against her son.

Gerðr. A giantess, daughter of the giant Gymir. Seen by Freyr from Odin's high seat Hliðskjálf and desired with an intensity that consumes him. Refuses Skírnir's gifts and resists his threats before yielding to his magical curse. Her union with Freyr is understood as a sacred marriage between the fertility god and the earth.

Guðrún. The most enduring figure in the Völsung cycle. Wife of Sigurðr, then of Atli, mother of Hamðir and Sörli. Survives every catastrophe the cycle produces — Sigurðr's murder, her revenge on Atli, the burning of his hall — and sends her sons to their deaths at Jörmunrekkr's court. Her grief is the emotional center of the heroic poems.

Gunnarr. Elder of Guðrún's brothers, king of the Gjukungs. Obtains Brynhildr as his wife through Sigurðr's disguised intervention. Complicit in Sigurðr's murder. Refuses to tell Atli where the gold is hidden. Killed in Atli's snake-pit, playing his harp with his feet.

Hamðir. Son of Guðrún and Jónakr, brother of Sörli and half-brother of Erpr. Travels with Sörli to avenge their sister Svanhildr at Jörmunrekkr's court. Kills Erpr on the road in a misunderstanding that ensures the mission's failure. His final speech is the Poetic Edda's last word on the heroic ideal.

Heimdallr. The divine watcher, guardian of the gods' realm, stationed at the Bifröst bridge. Possesses extraordinary sight and hearing. At Ragnarök he sounds the Gjallarhorn to summon the gods to battle. Kills Loki, and is killed by Loki, simultaneously.

Helgi Hundingsbane (*Helgi Hundingsbani*). The hero of the *Helgakviða Hundingsbana* poems. Born with his destiny pre-established by the nornir, loved by the valkyrie Sigrún who chooses him from the sky. Killed by Dagr, Sigrún's brother. Returns briefly from the dead to visit Sigrún in his burial mound, then departs permanently.

Höðr. The blind god, Baldr's brother. Unknowingly kills Baldr with a mistletoe dart guided by Loki. Killed by Váli in revenge. Returns with Baldr after Ragnarök in the renewed world, reconciled.

Högni. Guðrún's brother, steadiest of the Gjukungs. His heart is cut from his living body by Atli's men; he laughs as it is removed, demonstrating it is truly his and not the coward's heart previously offered as a deception.

Jörmungandr (*Miðgarðsormr*). The World Serpent, son of Loki and Angrboða. Encircles Miðgarðr at the bottom of the ocean, biting its own tail. Mortal enemy of Thor, who encounters it in the *Hymiskviða* before their fated mutual destruction at Ragnarök.

Loki. The trickster, shape-shifter, blood-brother of Odin. Son of the giant Fárbauti, admitted to the divine community by virtue of his cleverness. Father of Fenrir, Jörmungandr, and Hel by the giantess Angrboða; father of Sleipnir by the stallion Svaðilfari. Engineers Baldr's death, is captured and bound by the gods, breaks free at Ragnarök to lead the giants' fleet.

Níðhöggr. The serpent or dragon who gnaws at the root of Yggdrasill in Niflheim. Still alive after Ragnarök, flying over the renewed world with bodies in its wings — the *Völuspá*'s most ambiguous image of what survives catastrophe.

Njörðr. Vanir god of the sea, fishing, and coastal prosperity. Father of Freyr and Freyja. Married to the giantess Skaði in an arrangement that suits neither — she cannot tolerate his coastal home, he cannot tolerate her mountain hall.

Nornir. The three weavers of fate: Urð (that which was), Verðandi (that which is becoming), Skuld (that which shall be). They sit at the well of Urðr at the base of Yggdrasill and carve the destinies of gods and humans. They are not agents of divine will — they read and record the pattern already inherent in the structure of things.

Odin (*Óðinn*). The Allfather, chief of the Æsir, god of wisdom, war, poetry, death, and magic. Gave his eye to Mímir for wisdom. Hanged himself on Yggdrasill for nine nights to win the runes. Travels constantly in disguise, accumulating knowledge and managing the fates of warriors. Will be swallowed by Fenrir at Ragnarök.

Reginn. The dwarf-smith who fosters Sigurðr and guides him toward the killing of Fáfnir. His real motive is the gold that Fáfnir guards. Plans to betray Sigurðr after the dragon is killed. Killed by Sigurðr when the birds warn the hero of the plan.

Sigurðr. The greatest hero in the Norse tradition. Son of Sigmundr, foster-son of Reginn. Kills Fáfnir, acquires the cursed gold, wakes Sigrdrífa on Hindarfjall, is given a forgetting-potion by Grímhildr, marries Guðrún, is killed by Guttormr at Brynhildr's instigation. The Norse equivalent of Siegfried in the German tradition.

Skaði. Giantess, daughter of Þjazi. Comes to Ásgarðr armed for revenge after her father's death. Settles for compensation: a husband chosen from the gods (she receives Njörðr, having hoped for Baldr), and her father's eyes thrown into the sky as stars. Patron of hunting, skiing, and winter.

Snorri Sturluson. Not a mythological figure but essential context: the Icelandic historian and poet (1179–1241) who wrote the Prose Edda. His work is the primary secondary source for Norse mythology and the "manual" that drew on the Poetic Edda's mythological content. Reading the Poetic Edda is in part a process of going behind Snorri to his sources.

Thor (*Þórr*). Son of Odin, god of thunder, storms, and the protection of Miðgarðr. Wields the hammer Mjölnir. Worshipped particularly by farmers and ordinary people. His battles with giants are the subject of numerous poems; his mutual destruction with Jörmungandr at Ragnarök is one of the tradition's most precisely foretold fated outcomes.

Týr. God of justice, law, and single combat. Lost his right hand to Fenrir's jaws when the gods tricked the wolf into accepting the binding Gleipnir. The sacrifice of his hand guaranteed the binding that keeps Fenrir contained until Ragnarök.

Völva. Not a single figure but a type: the seeress who practices seiðr, moves between communities as an itinerant specialist, and communicates knowledge from beyond ordinary human perception. The speaker of the *Völuspá*, unnamed, is the corpus's supreme example. Her authority comes from her position outside the ordinary social order — powerful, necessary, and not quite safe.

Yggdrasill. The World Tree, an immense ash that connects the nine worlds of the Norse cosmos. Its three roots reach toward the Æsir, toward the frost giants (where Mímir's well lies), and toward Niflheim (where Níðhöggr gnaws from below). Its inhabitants include the eagle at the crown, the hawk Veðrfölnir, the squirrel Ratatoskr, four stags, and innumerable serpents.

Appendix B — Guide to the Poems

The Poetic Edda as preserved in the Codex Regius contains forty-five poems, or the remains of forty-five poems. Additional material survives in other manuscripts, principally AM 748 and the Hauksbók. What follows is a systematic guide to the major poems of the corpus: their Old Norse titles, their English equivalents, their manuscript homes, their approximate dating, and whether they receive extended treatment in this book.

The dating given here is necessarily approximate. Most poems cannot be dated with precision; the ranges reflect current scholarly consensus, which is itself contested.

"Ninth to tenth century" means the poem shows linguistic and stylistic features consistent with that period, not that we know when it was composed.

The Mythological Poems

Völuspá — The Prophecy of the Seeress. Codex Regius and Hauksbók. Late tenth to early eleventh century. Sixty-six stanzas in the Codex Regius version; the Hauksbók preserves a slightly longer text with significant variants. The most important poem in the corpus, covering the creation of the world, the first war between the gods, the death of Baldr, Ragnarök, and the world's renewal. Treated at length in Chapter 5.

Hávamál — The Words of the High One. Codex Regius. Composite text; individual sections range from the ninth to the twelfth century. One hundred and sixty-four stanzas, making it the longest poem in the corpus. Contains the Gnomic Verses, the Rúnatal, the Ljóðatal, the Loddfáfnismál, and the narrative episodes involving Billingr's daughter and Gunnlöðr. Treated at length in Chapter 6.

Vafþrúðnismál — The Sayings of Vafþrúðnir. Codex Regius. Tenth century. Fifty-five stanzas. A wisdom contest between Odin and the giant Vafþrúðnir, serving as a vehicle for systematic cosmological instruction. Treated in Chapter 7.

Grímnismál — The Lay of Grímnir. Codex Regius. Tenth to eleventh century. Fifty-four stanzas. Odin, tortured between two fires by a faithless king, delivers a catalogue of the divine dwellings, the World Tree, and his own names. Treated in Chapter 8.

Skírnismál — The Lay of Skírnir. Codex Regius. Tenth to eleventh century. Forty-two stanzas. Freyr's servant Skírnir courts the giantess Gerðr on his master's behalf, culminating in the tamsvísur, the most sustained piece of curse magic in the corpus. Treated in Chapter 9.

Hymiskviða — The Lay of Hymir. Codex Regius. Tenth to eleventh century. Thirty-nine stanzas. Thor and Týr travel to the hall of the giant Hymir to obtain a brewing cauldron; includes Thor's near-encounter with Jörmungandr. Treated in Chapter 10.

Lokasenna — Loki's Flyting. Codex Regius. Tenth to eleventh century. Sixty-six stanzas plus prose frame. Loki systematically insults the assembled gods at Ægir's feast, exposing the contradictions between their self-presentation and their actual conduct. Treated in Chapter 11.

Þrymskviða — The Lay of Þrymr. Codex Regius. Ninth to tenth century. Thirty-two stanzas. Thor, disguised as a bride, retrieves his stolen hammer Mjölnir from the giant Þrymr. The most comic poem in the corpus. Treated in Chapter 10.

Völundarkviða — The Lay of Völundr. Codex Regius. Ninth to tenth century. Forty-one stanzas plus prose frame. The elf-prince Völundr, captured and mutilated by a king, takes a methodical revenge before escaping on wings of his own forging. Treated in Chapter 12.

Alvíssmál — The Sayings of Alvíss. Codex Regius. Eleventh to twelfth century. Thirty-five stanzas. Thor detains the dwarf Alvíss through a night of questions about the names different beings give to things in the cosmos, until dawn turns Alvíss to stone. Not treated separately in this book; discussed briefly in the context of Chapter 4.

Baldrs draumar — Baldr's Dreams. AM 748. Tenth to eleventh century. Fourteen stanzas. Odin rides to Hel and raises a dead völva to prophesy about Baldr's fate. A short but significant poem; touched on in Chapters 5 and 7.

Rígsþula — The Lay of Ríg. AM 748. Tenth to eleventh century. Forty-nine stanzas. The god Heimdallr, traveling under the name Ríg, fathers the three classes of humanity — thrall, farmer, and noble. Not treated separately in this book.

Hyndluljóð — The Lay of Hyndla. Flateyjarbók. Eleventh to twelfth century. Fifty stanzas, including the embedded Völuspá in skamma (Short Völuspá). Freyja and the giantess Hyndla dispute the genealogy of the hero Óttar. Not treated separately in this book.

Svipdagsmál — The Lay of Svipdag. AM 748 and other sources. Date uncertain, possibly late. Composite of two poems, Gróugaldr and Fjölsvinnsmál. A hero uses his dead mother's magic and undergoes trials to reach an imprisoned woman. Not treated separately in this book.

Grottasöngr — The Song of Grotti. Codex Regius (appended to Skáldskaparmál). Ninth to tenth century. Twenty-four stanzas. Two giantess-slaves grind out peace, gold, and ultimately the doom of the king who overworks them. Not treated separately in this book.

The Heroic Poems

Helgakviða Hundingsbana I — The First Lay of Helgi Hundingsbane. Codex Regius. Tenth to eleventh century. Fifty-six stanzas. The birth, battles, and early love of Helgi and the valkyrie Sigrún. Treated in Chapter 14.

Helgakviða Hundingsbana II — The Second Lay of Helgi Hundingsbane. Codex Regius. Tenth to eleventh century. Fifty-one stanzas plus prose. Helgi's death and his return from the burial mound. Treated in Chapter 14.

Helgakviða Hjörvarðssonar — The Lay of Helgi Hjörvarðsson. Codex Regius. Tenth to eleventh century. Forty-three stanzas plus prose. A separate Helgi tradition, structured around the same valkyrie-choice pattern as the Hundingsbane poems. Treated in Chapter 14.

Grípisspá — The Prophecy of Grípir. Codex Regius. Probably eleventh to twelfth century (later than the other Sigurðr poems). Fifty-three stanzas. Sigurðr's uncle Grípir prophesies his nephew's entire life in advance. Treated in Chapter 15.

Reginsmál — The Lay of Reginn. Codex Regius. Tenth century. Twenty-six stanzas plus prose. The backstory of Andvari's cursed gold; Sigurðr's upbringing under the dwarf Reginn. Treated in Chapter 15.

Fáfnismál — The Lay of Fáfnir. Codex Regius. Tenth century. Forty-four stanzas plus prose. Sigurðr kills the dragon Fáfnir; dialogue with the dying dragon; the birds' warnings about Reginn's betrayal. Treated in Chapter 15.

Sigrdrífumál — The Lay of Sigrdrífa. Codex Regius (incomplete due to the lacuna). Tenth century. Fragment of approximately twenty-nine stanzas. Sigurðr wakes the valkyrie Sigrdrífa, who teaches him the runes. Treated in Chapter 15.

Brot af Sigurðarkviðu — Fragment of a Sigurðr Lay. Codex Regius. Tenth century. Sixteen stanzas, all that survived the lacuna. Covers the aftermath of Sigurðr's death from Brynhildr's perspective. Treated in Chapter 16.

Guðrúnarkviða I — The First Lay of Guðrún. Codex Regius. Tenth century. Twenty-seven stanzas. Guðrún's grief over Sigurðr's body; the hand on the dead face. Treated in Chapter 16.

Sigurðarkviða in skamma — The Short Lay of Sigurðr. Codex Regius. Tenth century. Seventy-one stanzas. The most complete single account of the events surrounding Sigurðr's death, told largely from Brynhildr's perspective. Treated in Chapter 16.

Helreið Brynhildar — Brynhildr's Ride to Hel. Codex Regius. Tenth century. Fourteen stanzas. Brynhildr, riding dead toward Hel, defends her life's choices to a hostile giantess. Treated in Chapter 16.

Guðrúnarkviða II — The Second Lay of Guðrún. Codex Regius. Tenth to eleventh century. Forty-four stanzas. Guðrún in exile tells her story from the beginning. Treated briefly in Chapter 16.

Guðrúnarkviða III — The Third Lay of Guðrún. Codex Regius. Tenth to eleventh century. Eleven stanzas. Guðrún undergoes a trial by ordeal. Treated briefly in Chapter 16.

Oddrúnargrátr — The Lament of Oddrún. Codex Regius. Tenth to eleventh century. Thirty-four stanzas. Atli's sister Oddrún laments her forbidden love for Gunnarr. Treated in Chapter 17.

Atlakviða — The Lay of Atli. Codex Regius. Ninth to tenth century (considered one of the oldest poems in the corpus). Forty-three stanzas. The destruction of the Gjukungs at Atli's court; Guðrún's total revenge. Treated in Chapter 17.

Atlamál in grœnlenzku — The Greenlandic Lay of Atli. Codex Regius. Eleventh to twelfth century. One hundred and five stanzas. An expanded, novelistic retelling of the same events as the Atlakviða. Treated in Chapter 17.

Guðrúnarhvöt — Guðrún's Incitement. Codex Regius. Tenth century. Twenty-one stanzas. Guðrún urges her sons Hamðir and Sörli to avenge their sister Svanhildr. A brief poem connecting the Atlakviða cycle to the Hamðismál.

Hamðismál — The Lay of Hamðir. Codex Regius. Ninth to tenth century (possibly the oldest poem in the corpus). Thirty stanzas. Hamðir and Sörli travel to avenge Svanhildr at the court of the Gothic king Jörmunrekkr. Treated in Chapter 18.

Appendix C — Which Translation Should You Read?

There is no perfect translation of the Poetic Edda. Every translator makes different sacrifices — between fidelity to the original meter and readability in English, between literal accuracy and poetic effect, between scholarly apparatus and accessibility. The translations described here are the best currently available in English, followed by two free versions accessible online. Each one is the right choice for a different kind of reader.

Carolyne Larrington. The Poetic Edda. Oxford World's Classics, revised edition 2014.

The most widely used translation in university courses and the most accessible entry point for general readers. Larrington's prose is clean and modern, her notes are helpful without being overwhelming, and her introduction provides solid historical and literary context. She does not attempt to reproduce the alliterative structure of the original, which means the verse reads more like prose poetry than like Old Norse verse — but for readers coming to the material for the first time, this is a reasonable trade. The revised 2014 edition incorporates significant improvements over the original 1996 version. Best for: first-time readers, students, anyone who wants a reliable and readable general introduction to the corpus.

Jackson Crawford. The Poetic Edda: Stories of the Norse Gods and Heroes. Hackett Publishing, 2015.

The most contemporary-sounding translation available, written in a colloquial modern English that makes the poems immediately accessible to readers with no background in the tradition. Crawford is a scholar who also works as a communicator, and his translation reflects both qualities — it is accurate, it is engaging, and it is the version most used in modern Asatru communities. The colloquial register occasionally loses some of the gravity of the more archaic passages, but gains significantly in immediacy. Best for: modern practitioners, casual readers, anyone who finds other translations stiff or remote.

Andy Orchard. The Elder Edda: A Book of Viking Lore. Penguin Classics, 2011.

The translation that pays the most attention to the poems as poems. Orchard makes a sustained attempt to reproduce the alliterative patterns of the original in English, giving his version a texture closer to what the original verse actually sounded like. More demanding than the others, but consistently rewarding for readers willing to slow down and let its rhythms accumulate. His introduction is substantial and excellent. Best for: readers with some existing familiarity with the tradition, anyone interested in the formal qualities of the poetry as verse.

Free Online Access

Two complete translations of the Poetic Edda are freely available online and can be read on any device.

Henry Adams Bellows (1936). The best of the public domain translations — complete, annotated, and more readable than most of its contemporaries. Available at sacred-texts.com/neu/poe/index.htm and on Project Gutenberg. The copyright was not renewed and the text is now free to access and share. A solid choice for readers who want the full corpus without the cost of a printed edition.

Edward Pettit (2023). The most significant recent addition to the field and, remarkably, fully open-access. Published by Open Book Publishers, this is the first single-volume parallel edition presenting the Old Norse text alongside a modern English translation, with introductions, synopses, and notes for each poem. It is the closest thing currently available to a definitive scholarly edition that any reader can access without cost.

Scan to read either translation in full, for free:

Henry Adams Bellows (1936)

Edward Pettit (2023)

A practical note: there is no reason to read only one translation. Reading the same passage in Larrington and Crawford side by side, or comparing either with the Pettit, will teach you more about what the original is doing than any single version can provide alone. The differences between translations are themselves a form of commentary on the poems.

Thanks

If this book has been useful to you — if it has given you a clearer sense of what the Poetic Edda is, what these poems were doing a thousand years ago, and why they are still worth reading today — I would be genuinely grateful if you took a few minutes to leave a review on Amazon.

Reviews make an enormous difference for independent authors. They help other readers find the book, and they help me understand what is resonating and what could be better. A sentence or two about what you found valuable is more than enough. Your words carry more weight than you might expect.

Thank you for making this journey with me — from the void before creation to the new green earth that rises after Ragnarök, from the völva's first words to Hamðir's last. I hope it has left you with a genuine curiosity about this tradition, and perhaps with the sense that these voices, however old and however fragmentary, are still saying something that needed to be said.

Skol.

Erik Hansen

www.ingramcontent.com/pod-product-compliance
Lightning Source LLC
Chambersburg PA
CBHW051540050726
47595CB00002B/574

* 9 7 8 1 9 7 1 7 6 1 0 4 6 *